# Cybercrime

# Other Books in the Issues on Trial Series:

# Cybercrime

*Sylvia Engdahl, Book Editor*

**GREENHAVEN PRESS**
*A part of Gale, Cengage Learning*

GALE
CENGAGE Learning™

Detroit • New York • San Francisco • New Haven, Conn • Waterville, Maine • London

GALE
CENGAGE Learning

Christine Nasso, *Publisher*
Elizabeth Des Chenes, *Managing Editor*

© 2010 Greenhaven Press, a part of Gale, Cengage Learning

*For more information, contact:*
Greenhaven Press
27500 Drake Rd.
Farmington Hills, MI 48331-3535
Or you can visit our Internet site at gale.cengage.com.

For product information and technology assistance, contact us at

Gale Customer Support, 1-800-877-4253
For permission to use material from this text or product, submit all requests online at www.cengage.com/permissions

Further permissions questions can be emailed to permissionrequest@cengage.com

Articles in Greenhaven Press anthologies are often edited for length to meet page requirements. In addition, original titles of these works are changed to clearly present the main thesis and to explicitly indicate the author's opinion. Every effort is made to ensure that Greenhaven Press accurately reflects the original intent of the authors. Every effort has been made to trace the owners of copyrighted material.

Cover photograph reproduced by permission of Nicholas Kamm/AFP/Getty Images.

**LIBRARY OF CONGRESS CATALOGING-IN-PUBLICATION DATA**

Cybercrime / Sylvia Engdahl, book editor.
    p. cm. -- (Issues on trial)
  Includes bibliographical references and index.
  ISBN-13: 978-0-7377-4487-3 (hardcover)
  1. Computer crimes--United States--Juvenile literature. I. Engdahl, Sylvia.
  KF390.5.C6C922 2009
  345.73'0268--dc22

                                                        2009019789

Printed in the United States of America
1 2 3 4 5 6 7 13 12 11 10 09

# Contents

## Chapter 1: ISPs Need Not Reveal Identities of Peer-to-Peer File Sharers

# Chapter 2: The Counterhacking of a Computer to Protect a Network Is Constitutional

## Chapter 3: Cybercrimes Committed in One State Can Be Prosecuted by Another

## Chapter 4: Prohibition of Internet Offerings of Child Pornography Is Constitutional

# Foreword

The U.S. courts have long served as a battleground for the most highly charged and contentious issues of the time. Divisive matters are often brought into the legal system by activists who feel strongly for their cause and demand an official resolution. Indeed, subjects that give rise to intense emotions or involve closely held religious or moral beliefs lay at the heart of the most polemical court rulings in history. One such case was *Brown v. Board of Education* (1954), which ended racial segregation in schools. Prior to *Brown*, the courts had held that blacks could be forced to use separate facilities as long as these facilities were equal to that of whites.

For years many groups had opposed segregation based on religious, moral, and legal grounds. Educators produced heartfelt testimony that segregated schooling greatly disadvantaged black children. They noted that in comparison to whites, blacks received a substandard education in deplorable conditions. Religious leaders such as Martin Luther King Jr. preached that the harsh treatment of blacks was immoral and unjust. Many involved in civil rights law, such as Thurgood Marshall, called for equal protection of all people under the law, as their study of the Constitution had indicated that segregation was illegal and un-American. Whatever their motivation for ending the practice, and despite the threats they received from segregationists, these ardent activists remained unwavering in their cause.

Those fighting against the integration of schools were mainly white southerners who did not believe that whites and blacks should intermingle. Blacks were subordinate to whites, they maintained, and society had to resist any attempt to break down strict color lines. Some white southerners charged that segregated schooling was *not* hindering blacks' education. For example, Virginia attorney general J. Lindsay Almond as-

serted, "With the help and the sympathy and the love and respect of the white people of the South, the colored man has
risen under that educational process to a place of eminence
and respect throughout the nation. It has served him well." So
when the Supreme Court ruled against the segregationists in
*Brown*, the South responded with vociferous cries of protest.
Even government leaders criticized the decision. The governor
of Arkansas, Orval Faubus, stated that he would not "be a
party to any attempt to force acceptance of change to which
the people are so overwhelmingly opposed." Indeed, resistance
to integration was so great that when black students arrived at
the formerly all-white Central High School in Arkansas, federal troops had to be dispatched to quell a threatening mob of
protesters.

Nevertheless, the *Brown* decision was enforced and the
South integrated its schools. In this instance, the Court, while
not settling the issue to everyone's satisfaction, functioned as
an instrument of progress by forcing a major social change.
Historian David Halberstam observes that the *Brown* ruling
"deprived segregationist practices of their moral legitimacy. . . .
It was therefore perhaps the single most important moment
of the decade, the moment that separated the old order from
the new and helped create the tumultuous era just arriving."
Considered one of the most important victories for civil rights,
*Brown* paved the way for challenges to racial segregation in
many areas, including on public buses and in restaurants.

In examining *Brown*, it becomes apparent that the courts
play an influential role—and face an arduous challenge—in
shaping the debate over emotionally charged social issues.
Judges must balance competing interests, keeping in mind the
high stakes and intense emotions on both sides. As exempli-
fied by *Brown*, judicial decisions often upset the status quo
and initiate significant changes in society. Greenhaven Press's
Issues on Trial series captures the controversy surrounding influential court rulings and explores the social ramifications of

such decisions from varying perspectives. Each anthology highlights one social issue—such as the death penalty, students' rights, or wartime civil liberties. Each volume then focuses on key historical and contemporary court cases that helped mold the issue as we know it today. The books include a compendium of primary sources—court rulings, dissents, and immediate reactions to the rulings—as well as secondary sources from experts in the field, people involved in the cases, legal analysts, and other commentators opining on the implications and legacy of the chosen cases. An annotated table of contents, an in-depth introduction, and prefaces that overview each case all provide context as readers delve into the topic at hand. To help students fully probe the subject, each volume contains book and periodical bibliographies, a comprehensive index, and a list of organizations to contact. With these features, the Issues on Trial series offers a well-rounded perspective on the courts' role in framing society's thorniest, most impassioned debates.

# Introduction

Just what is cybercrime? Sometimes it is defined as any crime that is committed using a computer or network of computers. On the other hand, it may be said to encompass only crimes for which the use of a computer is necessary, excluding crimes like fraud that can also be committed by other means. In practice, the line between ordinary crime and cybercrime is generally drawn somewhere between these extremes. Most people think of cybercrime as crime that is committed in cyberspace—that is, on the Internet or some other computer network, apart from any offline contact between perpetrator and victim—although there are a few cases where a single computer, such as a stolen one, could be involved.

The U.S. Department of Justice places cybercrimes in three categories:

- **The computer as a target** (using a computer to attack other computers, for example by hacking or distributing malware)

- **The computer as a weapon** (using a computer to commit crimes that can also be committed offline, such as fraud, theft, or harassment)

- **The computer as an accessory** (using a computer to store illegal files or information, such as pirated music or child pornography)

Everyone agrees that cybercrime is a growing problem. Just as computers and the Internet have given more and more capabilities to ordinary citizens than were available in the past, they have given more to criminals as well. Before the Internet existed, there were crooks who operated scams, but individually they could cheat relatively few people. Now each one can contact millions of potential victims. There were thieves who found ways to steal money, but they could not tap the bank balances of thousands of unsuspecting people, as is possible now. There were people who shoplifted CDs, but they could not steal hundreds of copyrighted recordings without going near a store, as has become common practice today.

Furthermore, as governments, businesses, and individuals have become increasingly dependent on computers and computer networks to conduct their regular activities, the danger of disruption of those activities by attackers has been greatly magnified. Once, altering or destroying the vital records of an organization required physical access to them. Now it can be done from anywhere in the world simply by malicious programming. Maintaining the security of computers systems has become a crucial concern of all organizations, and even of ordinary home users who have no particular reason to be considered targets. In addition to cybercriminals seeking to profit, some attack merely to show off their skills. Never before in history have average citizens needed to be on constant guard against the likely invasion of their private lives by strangers. There was, to be sure, some danger of becoming the victim of a mugger or a burglar, but the chances of this were small compared to the chances of a person who is not cautious online being victimized by scammers, identity thieves, or even sexual predators.

Identity theft is the worst of the cybercrimes against individuals, and it is not just adults with good credit ratings who need to worry about it. The Federal Trade Commission (FTC) estimates that more than four hundred thousand children have their identity stolen every year. Cybercriminals obtain access to their birth certificates and run up debts in their names; the victims often do not find out until long afterward, when they are denied employment or college loans, or find themselves unable to get driver's licenses on the grounds that someone already has a license with their social security number. They may even be arrested for crimes they did not commit.

So the risk of attracting sexual predators is not the only reason why it is important to keep identifying information about children off the Internet.

At present, cybercrime is out of control. A 2008 report commissioned by McAfee, a large security technology company, states that law enforcement is not yet effective against it because the police in most areas have been unable to keep up with the digital age. "There are mountains of digital evidence out there; the problem is that there aren't enough well-trained investigators, prosecutors and judges to use it effectively," said Peter Sommer, a professor at the London School of Economics.

Matthew Bevan, a reformed hacker also quoted in the McAfee report, agrees. He said, "I don't think law enforcement is equipped to deal with cybercrime, and this has always been the case, as people who love IT [information technology] and have the right skills go into IT jobs, not a law enforcement role. It is extremely rare that an IT specialist would join the police. Therefore, law enforcers lack the right skills to interpret cybercrime and know what to look for."

Another difficulty in combating cybercrime is the matter of jurisdiction. Most laws dealing with crime are state laws rather than federal laws. If a criminal in one state victimizes someone in another, or in many states, who has the authority to prosecute? This question is being worked out state by state in connection with specific cases, and some people feel federal laws will be necessary to resolve it.

Jurisdiction is an even more serious problem with respect to transnational cybercrime, which is on the rise. Criminals sometimes avoid prosecution by operating from countries where their particular activities are not against the law or enforcement capabilities are low. On the other hand, cyber attacks often originate much closer to their victims than is commonly supposed, as it is easy for hackers to route communication through foreign computers, thereby concealing its true origin. Moreover, international cybercrime gangs organized somewhat like the Mafia are proliferating. Most experts believe treaties are needed to establish uniform definitions of specific crimes and facilitate their investigation across international borders. Mary Kirwan, an international lawyer, has expressed her view of what will happen if nations fail to give higher priority to fighting cybercrime: "The bad guys will inherit the earth, and we will be left swinging in the wind."

Besides the major crimes being committed by gangs for financial gain, some people are using the Internet in harmful ways that are not now considered cybercrimes, but perhaps ought to be. One case that attracted wide media attention in 2008 was that of Lori Drew. Her teenage daughter had a falling out with another teen, Megan Meier, and so Ms. Drew created a fake MySpace account under the name of an imaginary boy, Josh Evans, which she used to harass Megan. Eventually, hurtful messages from "Josh Evans" caused Megan to commit suicide, and some time later Lori Drew was charged in federal court with a felony. As no existing law precisely covered the situation, the prosecutor maintained that violating the MySpace terms of service was the equivalent of hacking. The jury deadlocked on that charge, but convicted Lori Drew of obtaining unauthorized access to MySpace, a misdemeanor. Most legal experts were dismayed by the hacking charge, which they said would make anyone who violated any Web site's terms of service a felon. But bloggers as well as people in Lori Drew's neighborhood called her a murderer and were upset by the verdict. The issue of whether cyberbullying should be made a crime remains controversial. Many believe that it should, while others feel the effect on free speech would be too great.

Usually, when a cybercrime case reaches court, the matter to be decided is merely whether or not the defendant is guilty. Therefore, relatively few such cases are appealed to higher courts, which are concerned with the interpretation or constitutionality of laws. The U.S. Supreme Court has reviewed only two, both concerned with laws against distribution of child pornography on the Internet—one of which is included in this book. The other cases included are federal circuit court or state court cases. They are examples of the questions that are being raised about differences between cybercrime and other crime. Many more such questions are likely to arise in the years to come.

# CHAPTER 1

# ISPs Need Not Reveal Identities of Peer-to-Peer File Sharers

# Case Overview

## *Recording Industry Association of America v. Verizon Internet Services* (2003)

Ever since broadband access to the Internet became available, the recording industry has been trying to stop the illegal sharing of copyrighted music files. In the 1990s Internet service providers (ISPs) were worried because under traditional copyright law, they might be held liable for contributing to copyright infringement by their users, so they asked Congress to pass legislation that would protect them. The result was the Digital Millennium Copyright Act (DMCA) of 1998, which was based on compromises worked out after long negotiations with the ISP industry and organizations representing copyright owners. Under the DMCA, ISPs are not liable for conduct by their users that they have no way of detecting, but if a copyright holder identifies illegal copies, it can force the ISP to remove them from its servers and provide the name of the user involved so that he or she can be sued.

This works well when unauthorized copies are located at a Web site. An early file-sharing site, Napster, stored a great many files illegally and was shut down after a federal court ruling. But file sharing continued through peer-to-peer (P2P) networks that do not store any files on the ISP's server. In a P2P network, files are transmitted directly from one user's computer to another. The DMCA protects ISPs from copyright infringement liability when it merely transmit files without storing them. However, the Recording Industry Association of America (RIAA) believed that even then it could send subpoenas to ISPs demanding the names of illegal file sharers.

At first no one questioned this. The RIAA, having had little success in combating P2P networks directly, decided to sue as many individual file sharers as possible. It sent subpoenas to their ISPs, some of which agreed to provide the names, and several hundred suits were filed, including one against a user who turned out to be a twelve-year-old girl.

But one ISP, Verizon, refused to reveal users' identities. It held that this would violate their privacy, their First Amendment right to communicate anonymously, and the Constitution's due process clause. Also, Verizon's lawyers took a closer look at the wording of the DMCA. They discovered that among other requirements specified in the section authorizing the sending of subpoenas, a copyright holder must identify copyrighted material to be removed from the ISP's servers. When no such material is stored on its server, this requirement cannot be met. Therefore, Verizon said, RIAA subpoenas demanding the identities of P2P file sharers are not legal and ISPs need not comply with them.

The lower court rejected this argument and ordered Verizon to disclose the names. A U.S. court of appeals, however, decided that Verizon's interpretation was correct. It ruled that there was no need to consider the issue of constitutionality because the law clearly excludes P2P file sharing, which had not yet been invented when the DMCA was passed. Although the RIAA argued that this is a mere technicality and that Congress undoubtedly intended the DMCA to apply to all illegal file sharing regardless of where the files are stored, the court did not have the power to rewrite the law to fit new Internet technology. Only Congress can do that.

Verizon maintained from the beginning that "it's about privacy, not piracy," and was supported by many public interests and privacy organizations. It won the case, but the RIAA has since filed thousands of suits against file sharers, using a more complicated procedure that requires a judge to approve each subpoena. Many people believe that this is ineffective and that a better way to ensure payment for musicians should be found.

> "Nothing in the legislative history sup-
> ports the issuance of a ... subpoena to
> an ISP acting as a conduit for P2P file
> sharing."

# The Court's Opinion: ISPs Cannot Be Subpoenaed by Copyright Holders If They Do Not Store Illegal Copies

## Douglas H. Ginsburg

*Douglas H. Ginsburg is a judge on the United States Court of Appeals for the District of Columbia Circuit. He served as its chief judge from 2001 to 2008. In the following opinion in* RIAA v. Verizon, *he explains Verizon's and RIAA's differing interpretations of a provision of the Digital Millennium Copyright Act (DMCA) that permits copyright owners to force Internet service providers to reveal the names of copyright infringers. Verizon argued that this provision does not apply to peer-to-peer (P2P) file transfers, in which the files are not stored on its servers, while RIAA claimed that it does. The court decided that the wording of the law excludes P2P transfers and that there was no evidence that Congress intended it to cover new technologies unknown at the time the law was passed. Therefore, it ruled in Verizon's favor.*

This case concerns the Recording Industry Association of America's [RIAA] use of the subpoena provision of the Digital Millennium Copyright Act [DMCA], to identify inter-

Douglas H. Ginsburg, opinion, *Recording Industry Association of America v. Verizon Internet Services*, U.S. Court of Appeals for the District of Columbia, December 19, 2003. Reproduced by permission.

net users the RIAA believes are infringing the copyrights of its members. The RIAA served two subpoenas upon Verizon Internet Services in order to discover the names of two Verizon subscribers who appeared to be trading large numbers of .mp3 files of copyrighted music via "peer-to-peer" (P2P) file sharing programs, such as KaZaA. Verizon refused to comply with the subpoenas on various legal grounds.

The district court rejected Verizon's statutory and constitutional challenges to [the DMCA] and ordered the internet service provider (ISP) to disclose to the RIAA the names of the two subscribers. . . .

Because we agree with Verizon's interpretation of the statute, we reverse the orders of the district court enforcing the subpoenas and do not reach either of Verizon's constitutional arguments.

Individuals with a personal computer and access to the internet began to offer digital copies of recordings for download by other users, an activity known as file sharing, in the late 1990's using a program called Napster. Although recording companies and music publishers successfully obtained an injunction against Napster's facilitating the sharing of files containing copyrighted recordings, millions of people in the United States and around the world continue to share digital .mp3 files of copyrighted recordings using P2P computer programs such as KaZaA, Morpheus, Grokster, and eDonkey. Unlike Napster, which relied upon a centralized communication architecture to identify the .mp3 files available for download, the current generation of P2P file sharing programs allow an internet user to search directly the .mp3 file libraries of other users; no web site is involved. To date, owners of copyrights have not been able to stop the use of these decentralized programs.

The RIAA now has begun to direct its anti-infringement efforts against individual users of P2P file sharing programs. In order to pursue apparent infringers the RIAA needs to be able to identify the individuals who are sharing and trading files using P2P programs. The RIAA can readily obtain the screen name of an individual user, and using the Internet Protocol (IP) address associated with that screen name, can trace the user to his ISP. Only the ISP, however, can link the IP address used to access a P2P program with the name and address of a person—the ISP's customer—who can then be contacted or, if need be, sued by the RIAA.

The RIAA has used the subpoena provisions of Section 512(h) of the Digital Millennium Copyright Act (DMCA) to compel ISPs to disclose the names of subscribers whom the RIAA has reason to believe are infringing its members' copyrights. Some ISPs have complied with the RIAA's subpoenas and identified the names of the subscribers sought by the RIAA. The RIAA has sent letters to and filed lawsuits against several hundred such individuals, each of whom allegedly made available for download by other users hundreds or in some cases even thousands of .mp3 files of copyrighted recordings. Verizon refused to comply with and instead has challenged the validity of the two subpoenas it has received. . . .

## Verizon's Argument

On July 24, 2002 the RIAA served Verizon with a subpoena . . . , seeking the identity of a subscriber whom the RIAA believed to be engaged in infringing activity. The subpoena was for "information sufficient to identify the alleged infringer of the sound recordings described in the attached notification." The "notification of claimed infringement" identified the IP address of the subscriber and about 800 sound files he offered for trading; expressed the RIAA's "good faith belief" the file sharing activity of Verizon's subscriber constituted infringement of its members' copyrights; and asked for Verizon's "immediate assistance in stopping this unauthorized activity." "Specifically, we request that you remove or disable access to the infringing sound files via your system."

When Verizon refused to disclose the name of its subscriber, the RIAA filed a motion to compel production.... In opposition to that motion, Verizon argued Section 512(h) does not apply to an ISP acting merely as a conduit for an individual using a P2P file sharing program to exchange files. The district court rejected Verizon's argument based upon "the language and structure of the statute, as confirmed by the purpose and history of the legislation," and ordered Verizon to disclose to the RIAA the name of its subscriber....

The RIAA then obtained another subpoena directed to Verizon. This time Verizon moved to quash the subpoena, arguing that the district court, acting through the Clerk, lacked jurisdiction under Article III to issue the subpoena and in the alternative that Section 512(h) violates the First Amendment. The district court rejected Verizon's constitutional arguments, denied the motion to quash, and again ordered Verizon to disclose the identity of its subscriber....

The issue is whether Section 512(h) applies to an ISP acting only as a conduit for data transferred between two internet users, such as persons sending and receiving e-mail or, as in this case, sharing P2P files. Verizon contends Section 512(h) does not authorize the issuance of a subpoena to an ISP that transmits infringing material but does not store any such material on its servers. The RIAA argues Section 512(h) on its face authorizes the issuance of a subpoena to an "[internet] service provider" without regard to whether the ISP is acting as a conduit for user-directed communications. We conclude from both the terms of Section 512(h) and the overall structure of Section 512 that, as Verizon contends, a subpoena may be issued only to an ISP engaged in storing on its servers material that is infringing or the subject of infringing activity....

## What the Law Says

Section 512 creates four safe harbors, each of which immunizes ISPs from liability for copyright infringement under certain highly specified conditions. Subsection 512(a), entitled "Transitory digital network communications," provides a safe harbor "for infringement of copyright by reason of the [ISP's] transmitting, routing, or providing connections for" infringing material, subject to certain conditions, including that the transmission is initiated and directed by an internet user. Subsection 512(b), "System caching," provides immunity from liability "for infringement of copyright by reason of the intermediate and temporary storage of material on a system or network controlled or operated by or for the [ISP]," as long as certain conditions regarding the transmission and retrieval of the material created by the ISP are met. Subsection 512(c), "Information residing on systems or networks at the direction of users," creates a safe harbor from liability "for infringement of copyright by reason of the storage at the direction of a user of material that resides on a system or network controlled or operated by or for the service provider," as long as the ISP meets certain conditions regarding its lack of knowledge concerning, financial benefit from, and expeditious efforts to remove or deny access to, material that is infringing or that is claimed to be the subject of infringing activity. Finally, Subsection 512(d), "Information location tools," provides a safe harbor from liability "for infringement of copyright by reason of the provider referring or linking users to an online location containing infringing material or infringing activity, by using information location tools" such as "a directory, index, reference, pointer, or hypertext link," subject to the same conditions as in Subsections 512(c)(1)(a)-(c).

Notably present in Sections 512(b)-(d), and notably absent from Section 512(a), is the so-called notice and take-down provision. It makes a condition of the ISP's protection from liability for copyright infringement that "upon notification of claimed infringement . . ." the ISP "responds expeditiously to remove, or disable access to, the material that is claimed to be infringing."

Verizon argues that Section 512(h) by its terms precludes the Clerk of Court from issuing a subpoena to an ISP acting as a conduit for P2P communications because a Section 512(h) subpoena request cannot meet the requirement . . . that a proposed subpoena contain "a copy of a notification [of claimed infringement, . . ." In particular, Verizon maintains the two subpoenas obtained by the RIAA fail to meet the requirements . . . in that they do not—because Verizon is not storing the infringing material on its server—and can not, identify material "to be removed or access to which is to be disabled" by Verizon. . . .

Infringing material obtained or distributed via P2P file sharing is located in the computer (or in an off-line storage device, such as a compact disc) of an individual user. No matter what information the copyright owner may provide, the ISP can neither "remove" nor "disable access to" the infringing material because that material is not stored on the ISP's servers. Verizon can not remove or disable one user's access to infringing material resident on another user's computer because Verizon does not control the content on its subscribers' computers.

## RIAA's Argument

The RIAA contends an ISP can indeed "disable access" to infringing material by terminating the offending subscriber's internet account. This argument is undone by the terms of the Act, however. As Verizon notes, the Congress considered disabling an individual's access to infringing material and disabling access to the internet to be different remedies for the protection of copyright owners, the former blocking access to the infringing material on the offender's computer and the latter more broadly blocking the offender's access to the internet (at least via his chosen ISP). These distinct statutory remedies establish that terminating a subscriber's account is not the same as removing or disabling access by others to the infringing material resident on the subscriber's computer.

The RIAA points out that even if, with respect to an ISP functioning as a conduit for user-directed communications, a copyright owner cannot satisfy the requirement of . . . identifying material to be removed by the ISP, a notification is effective . . . if it "includes substantially" the required information; that standard is satisfied, the RIAA maintains, because the ISP can identify the infringer based upon the information provided by the copyright owner. . . . According to the RIAA, the purpose of Section 512(h) being to identify infringers, a notice should be deemed sufficient so long as the ISP can identify the infringer from the IP address in the subpoena.

Nothing in the Act itself says how we should determine whether a notification "includes substantially" all the required information; both the Senate and House Reports, however, state the term means only that "technical errors . . . such as misspelling a name" or "supplying an outdated area code" will not render ineffective an otherwise complete notification. Clearly, however, the defect in the RIAA's notification is not a mere technical error; nor could it be thought "insubstantial" even under a more forgiving standard. The RIAA's notification identifies absolutely no material Verizon could remove or access to which it could disable, which indicates to us that Section 512(c)(3)(A) concerns means of infringement other than P2P file sharing.

Finally, the RIAA argues the definition of "[internet] service provider" in Section 512(k)(1)(B) makes Section 512(h) applicable to an ISP regardless what function it performs with respect to infringing material—transmitting it per Section 512(a), caching it per Section 512(b), hosting it per Section 512(c), or locating it per Section 512(d).

This argument borders upon the silly. The details of this argument need not burden the Federal Reporter, for the specific provisions of Section 512(h), which we have just rehearsed, make clear that however broadly "[internet] service provider" is defined . . . , a subpoena may issue to an ISP only under the prescribed conditions regarding notification. Define all the world as an ISP if you like, the validity of a Section 512(h) subpoena still depends upon the copyright holder having given the ISP, however defined, a notification effective under Section 512(c)(3)(A). And as we have seen, any notice to an ISP concerning its activity as a mere conduit does not satisfy the condition . . . and is therefore ineffective. . . .

In support of its claim that Section 512(h) can—and should—be read to reach P2P technology, the RIAA points to congressional testimony and news articles available to the Congress prior to passage of the DMCA. These sources document the threat to copyright owners posed by bulletin board services (BBSs) and file transfer protocol (FTP) sites, which the RIAA says were precursors to P2P programs.

## What Congress Intended

We need not, however, resort to investigating what the 105th Congress may have known because the text of Section 512(h) and the overall structure of Section 512 clearly establish, as we have seen, that Section 512(h) does not authorize the issuance of a subpoena to an ISP acting as a mere conduit for the transmission of information sent by others. Legislative history can serve to inform the court's reading of an otherwise ambiguous text; it cannot lead the court to contradict the legislation itself.

In any event, not only is the statute clear (albeit complex), the legislative history of the DMCA betrays no awareness whatsoever that internet users might be able directly to exchange files containing copyrighted works. That is not surprising; P2P software was "not even a glimmer in anyone's eye when the DMCA was enacted." *In re Verizon I*. Furthermore, such testimony as was available to the Congress prior to passage of the DMCA concerned "hackers" who established unauthorized FTP or BBS sites on the servers of ISPs, rogue ISPs that posted FTP sites on their servers, thereby making files of copyrighted musical works available for download, and BBS subscribers using dial-up technology to connect to a BBS hosted by an ISP. The Congress had no reason to foresee the application of section 512(h) to P2P file sharing, nor did they draft the DMCA broadly enough to reach the new technology when it came along. Had the Congress been aware of P2P technology, or anticipated its development, Section 512(h) might have been drafted more generally. Be that as it may, contrary to the RIAA's claim, nothing in the legislative history supports the issuance of a Section 512(h) subpoena to an ISP acting as a conduit for P2P file sharing.

Finally, the RIAA argues Verizon's interpretation of the statute "would defeat the core objectives" of the Act. More specifically, according to the RIAA there is no policy justification for limiting the reach of Section 512(h) to situations in which the ISP stores infringing material on its system, considering that many more acts of copyright infringement are committed in the P2P realm, in which the ISP merely transmits the material for others, and that the burden upon an ISP required to identify an infringing subscriber is minimal.

We are not unsympathetic either to the RIAA's concern regarding the widespread infringement of its members' copyrights, or to the need for legal tools to protect those rights. It is not the province of the courts, however, to rewrite the DMCA in order to make it fit a new and unforeseen internet architecture, no matter how damaging that development has been to the music industry or threatens being to the motion picture and software industries. The plight of copyright holders must be addressed in the first instance by the Congress; only the "Congress has the constitutional authority and the institutional ability to accommodate fully the varied permutations of competing interests that are inevitably implicated by such new technology" *Sony Corp. v. Universal City Studios* (1984).

The stakes are large for the music, motion picture, and software industries and their role in fostering technological innovation and our popular culture. It is not surprising, therefore, that even as this case was being argued, committees of the Congress were considering how best to deal with the threat to copyrights posed by P2P file sharing schemes.

> *"Internet copyright piracy is the same regardless of whether the infringer utilizes a peer-to-peer service or distributes unauthorized digital copies over the Internet some other way."*

# Congress Intended the DMCA to Apply to All Illegal Internet Copying

*Paul B. Gaffney et al.*

*Paul B. Gaffney is a Washington, D.C., attorney who has represented the film industry in a number of lawsuits involving illegal copying. The following viewpoint is part of an amici curiae (friends of the court) brief—that is, a written legal argument of a person or organization not directly involved in a lawsuit that will be affected by its outcome—of which he was the lead author. Writing about the case RIAA v. Verizon on behalf of the Motion Picture Association of America, the American Federation of Musicians, and many other organizations concerned with the distribution of copyrighted works, Gaffney argues that widespread Internet piracy is a serious problem. The Digital Millennium Copyright Act (DMCA) provides a way for copyright holders to obtain the names of individual pirates from the pirates' Internet service providers (ISPs). But the ISP Verizon has refused to reveal the names, and has claimed that the DMCA does not apply to peer-to-peer (P2P) transfers, in which no copyright files*

Paul B. Gaffney et al., *Oral Argument, Nos. 03-7015, 03-7053*. Washington, DC: U.S. Court of Appeals for the District of Columbia Circuit, 2003. Reproduced by permission of the author.

*are stored on its server. Verizon's interpretation of the law is wrong, Gaffney says. He argues that Congress intended it to apply to all Internet piracy, regardless of where the files are stored.*

Underlying this appeal is the conduct of two customers of Verizon Internet Services ("Verizon") who are (or appear quite clearly to be) engaged in aggravated copyright infringement. One made 600 copyrighted recordings, the other 800 copyrighted recordings, available for download over his or her Verizon Internet connection. Each was utilizing one of the popular "peer-to-peer" services that in the present state of the Internet provide "the largest opportunity for copyright theft." *In re Verizon Internet Services.* These two individuals are inflicting damage on a very large scale, and their conduct is far from aberrant [atypical]. As the District Court found, "[t]he extent of copyright infringement and piracy of intellectual property over the Internet . . . is well-recognized and 'has reached epidemic proportions.'"

Both of these individuals remained anonymous to the victims of their copyright infringement until this Court's Order of June 4, 2003, which obligated Verizon to provide the Recording Industry Association of America (RIAA) with their identities. The issue in this appeal is whether and under what circumstances a copyright owner may utilize the procedural remedy Congress enacted to address this problem—the "Subpoena to identify infringer" provision enacted in [the Digital Millennium Copyright Act (DMCA)]. Verizon and its supporting *amici* [friends of the court], many of whom urged Congress to enact this statute, now urge the Court to invalidate or at least judicially narrow it. The *amici* who have joined this brief respectfully submit that this challenge be rejected and that the two decisions of the District Court be affirmed.

This brief of *amici curiae* is submitted on behalf of some of the principal victims of the piracy "epidemic" noted by the District Court and others. . . .

## Technology Brings Opportunities and Risks

We are in the infancy of a networked, digital society. The early benefits of this transformation are obvious to anyone who has replaced his or her VCR with a DVD player, downloaded or updated software products over the Internet, or sampled and purchased music without visiting a record store. New and exciting online markets for distributing legitimate content are becoming a reality every day, and with advances in technology there will be benefits we have not yet imagined. But with these opportunities come real risks. The Internet and the inexpensive-yet-powerful computers that people use to access it are technological marvels, but copyright pirates have employed the technology and the Internet to cause millions of dollars in harm to copyright owners. At no cost, and with just a few clicks of a mouse, these individuals can copy and disseminate virtually perfect copies of digital works—*e.g.*, motion pictures, musical recordings, software—on a global scale. Left unchecked, these copyright thieves threaten to destroy the legitimate digital marketplace for works of art, music, film, software, literature, and other video programming, and will deter the development and distribution of new works in state-of-the-art digital media. The Digital Millennium Copyright Act of 1998 (DMCA) was Congress's response to the threat and the reality of digital piracy. In this landmark law, Congress sought to make the risks of copyright infringement more manageable by giving those in the creative industries an incentive to produce and distribute works in digital formats by assuring them of reasonable and reliable procedural remedies. . . .

## Joint Responsibility

Congressional deliberations over the legislation continued for months. . . . The ISP [Internet service provider] industry acknowledged that the task of combating Internet copyright piracy would have to be one of "joint responsibility between copyright owners and ISPs." *Hearing* (prepared statement of Roy Neel). As this ISP industry representative stated, "When ISPs acquire actual knowledge that their services are being misused for infringing purposes, they should be obligated to take reasonable steps to halt further abuse."

> We believe that the task of ferreting out copyright infringement on the Internet should fall to the copyright owner. Today, copyright owners have access to a large array of Internet search engines and "spiders" to sniff out material they know belongs to them (unlike the ISPs, who cannot be certain who may have recently purchased which copyrighted material.) *Once the copyright owners discover infringement, they can bring it to the attention of the ISPs. It is at this point that the ISPs can sensibly act. . . .*

The final compromise reached by the parties was that "in exchange for the liability protections afforded to service providers in subsections (a) through (d) of [17 U.S.C. Section 512], Congress sought through subsection (h) to require service providers to assist copyright owners in identifying infringers using the service providers' systems." *First Subpoena Decision.*

While commonplace in 1998 when the DMCA was enacted, Internet copyright piracy had not yet reached the "epidemic proportions" that exist now. Nevertheless, that prospect was plainly on the mind of Congress as it was considering the legislation. The motion picture industry, for one, warned that rampant piracy of its product, while not then occurring, was inevitable as technology advanced:

> Movies and videos are not much in evidence yet. That is because the audio-visual content is so rich in information that it cannot yet move easily through the digital network. The volume of flow is simply too great for some of the pipes. But we also know that our present reprieve is only tempo-

rary. The same technology that will smooth the way for legitimate delivery of video on demand over digital networks will also prime the pump for copyright pirates.

*Hearing on S. 1146*, (testimony of Fritz Attaway). . . .

## Promotion of Digital Theft

This anticipated wave of digital theft has now crashed over the creative industries, facilitated by the provision of faster and faster Internet connections that, while providing enormous benefits for society, have also made it more practical for copyright pirates to copy and distribute large files, such as full-length motion pictures. (According to one recent study, the number of Americans who access the Internet from home via a broadband Internet connection grew 50 percent from March 2002 through March 2003 and has doubled since year-end 2001; an estimated 30 million Americans now have home broadband connections.) Many broadband users undoubtedly restrict their activities to lawful pursuits. Unfortunately, others do not. Driving this unlawful conduct are exactly the sort of Internet users whose identities were subpoenaed in this case. Under the cloak of anonymity, they sign on to peer-to-peer [P2P] file-copying services and offer for downloading numerous copies of the latest and most popular movies, recordings, and software. This conduct has continued to flourish notwithstanding a number of successful efforts by the recording and motion picture industries to shut down file-copying services that are not willing or capable of operating lawfully. . . .

While the success in litigating against peer-to-peer *services* has not been uniform, in every instance the courts have concluded without the slightest equivocation that *persons who use* these file-copying services to download copyrighted works and make them available to others—the very sort of individuals whose identity the RIAA seeks to learn in these proceedings—are engaged in direct copyright infringement. And there is no sign that this infringing conduct is abating. The company that provides the KaZaa file-copying service recently announced that 230 million copies of its software had been downloaded, making it (according to the company) the most popular free program on the Internet.

Regrettably, Verizon has revised its view of what it means to "act sensibly" in the face of this massive Internet piracy among its customers. To Verizon, "acting sensibly" apparently means finding a way to capitalize on and profit from the problem. An extraordinary piece of evidence submitted by Verizon itself to the District Court is promotional material for its broadband services. While the boilerplate in its customer service agreement states that use of its network for copyright infringement is strictly forbidden, Verizon in these marketing materials urges its customers to do just that. Verizon goes so far as to suggest that its broadband customers might want to bypass the licensed "official sites" that offer music downloads legally, and instead patronize the "free sites."

> [T]he official sites typically don't offer all music that is still selling exceedingly well in stores. *By contrast, the free sites are likely to have pretty much everything,* but you may well be pelted with some unwanted ads.

These promotional materials—in an "Essential Site List"— actually direct customers who are music lovers and "file-sharing fiends" to a peer-to-peer service named "Morpheus." Verizon now complements this pro-piracy marketing strategy with a legal strategy designed to impede the anti-piracy efforts it once vowed to aid.

## Safe Haven for Internet Pirates?

Verizon and its *amici* propose a construction of [the DMCA] that disowns the statutory compromise described above and that renders the "subpoena to identify infringer" virtually useless for its intended purpose.

Under this proposed construction, a copyright owner may not obtain a "subpoena to identify infringer" except where that individual stores his pirated catalogue on his ISP's computer, rather than his own computer. This construction would provide a safe haven for the vast majority of anonymous Internet pirates who increasingly utilize peer-to-peer services—services that, as the District Court noted (and Verizon does not dispute) provide "the largest opportunity for copyright theft." *First Subpoena Decision.* And this construction of [the DMCA] would for all practical purposes relieve ISPs of their obligation to assist anti-piracy efforts through the identification of customers suspected of infringement.

The District Court's thorough analysis rejecting this construction of the statute should be affirmed. Interpreting [the law] as inapplicable to peer-to-peer infringers like those at issue in this case "would create a huge loophole in Congress's effort to prevent copyright infringement on the Internet" and would "allow infringement to flourish." Verizon's alternative construction would violate the principle that "'absurd results' are strongly disfavored." *United States v. Wilson.* There is no dispute that the two individuals whose identities Verizon seeks to protect are engaged in "large-scale infringement activities." Nor is there any dispute that the only reliable way for one of the aggrieved copyright owners to secure their identities is through Verizon, their ISP. Verizon in turn has not claimed that its burden in identifying a particular peer-to-peer subscriber is any different or greater than identifying customers suspected of infringement by other means, such as those hosting materials on the ISP's server. As Verizon acknowledged below, the process of identifying the customer associated with that IP address takes only a few minutes. And, of course, the injury for which Congress was providing a remedy—Internet copyright piracy—is the same regardless of whether the infringer utilizes a peer-to-peer service or distributes unauthorized digital copies over the Internet some other way.

It is almost certainly true that, on an overall basis, Verizon and other ISPs will be subjected to more subpoenas if peer-to-peer infringers are subject to [the law]. That fact, however, cannot justify the invention of some otherwise non-existent legislative intent to carve out peer-to-peer infringers from the scope of the statute. It simply reflects the magnitude of the growing problem to which the statutory provision is addressed. Moreover, the burden on ISPs of complying with such subpoenas is still greatly outweighed by the benefit of being sheltered from monetary liability by the DMCA safe harbors.

There is nothing whatsoever in the statutory text or legislative record of the DMCA that might justify the embrace of Verizon's implausible interpretation of [the law]. Congress nowhere drew a distinction between peer-to-peer systems on the one hand, and on the other hand those circumstances where the ISP is providing (intentionally or unwittingly) a home for the infringer's pirated works. Nor was Congress acting out of ignorance of the potential problem, as Verizon suggests. To the contrary, the legislative materials reflect a discussion and awareness of the copyright piracy occurring outside of ISP servers, specifically among users of certain FTP (or file transfer protocol) sites, which functioned as a sort of early-stage peer-to-peer system. Had Congress wanted to limit these subpoenas to infringement hosted on ISP servers, as Verizon suggests, it could have done so simply and sensibly, by locating the subpoena provision within Section 512(c) [of the law], which provides other remedies for that particular problem. It did not do so, but rather made it a stand-alone provision that on its face applies to *all* "service providers." It may be that Congress in 1998 never anticipated the scope and extent of the copyright piracy that exists today, but there is no reason at all to believe that it preemptively circumscribed the application of one of the key tools it provided copyright owners to protect themselves. . . .

In the DMCA, Congress, after years of considering the competing issues involved, took on the latest threat to copyright—balancing the tremendous benefits of the Internet and digital technology against the very significant risks they pose to the intellectual property of present and future copyright owners. One cannot find in [the DMCA] the purported right to anonymity that Verizon invokes on behalf of the serial infringers at issue in this proceeding, and the others who are similarly inflicting massive injury on copyright owners. For the reasons set forth above, the Court should decline the invitation to create such a right. *Amici* respectfully submit that the Court should affirm the District Court's Orders.

*"Peer-to-peer [networks] did not exist when the DMCA was being drafted, and Congress did not have [the RIAA's] kind of subpoena factory in mind."*

# Congress Did Not Intend the DMCA to Apply to Peer-to-Peer Networks

## John Borland

*John Borland is a staff writer for CNET News. In the following article he explains that although in RIAA v. Verizon the federal appeals court ruled that copyright law does not allow the Recording Industry Association of America (RIAA) to send out subpoenas asking Internet service providers (ISPs) for the identity of file swappers, they will still be able to sue individuals for copyright infringement. It will merely slow down the process and reduce the number of lawsuits they can initiate. Verizon, which had appealed a lower court's decision in RIAA's favor, welcomed the new ruling as a protection of people's privacy on the Internet, while the RIAA claimed that it was inconsistent with what Congress intended when passing the Digital Millennium Copyright Act (DMCA). Borland argues, however, that the court held that the DMCA's provision for subpoenas does not apply to peer-to-peer (P2P) networks, in which files are transferred directly from one user to another, as P2P technology did not exist at the time the law was passed. Because the case involved only such networks, the court did not consider the issue of whether the DMCA subpoena procedure is unconstitutional.*

John Borland, "Court: RIAA Lawsuit Strategy Illegal," *CNET News*, December 19, 2003. Reproduced by permission.

A federal appeals court [in December 2003] handed a major setback to the record industry's legal tactics for tracking down and suing alleged file swappers, in a high-profile case pitting copyright law against the privacy rights of Internet users.

Reversing a series of decisions in favor of the Recording Industry Association of America (RIAA), the Washington, D.C., court said copyright law did not allow the group to send out subpoenas asking Internet service providers [ISPs] for the identity of file swappers on their networks without a judge's consent.

"We are not unsympathetic either to the RIAA's concern regarding the widespread infringement of its members' copyrights, or to the need for legal tools to protect those rights," the court wrote. "It is not the province of the courts, however, to rewrite [copyright law] in order to make it fit a new and unforeseen Internet architecture, no matter how damaging that development has been to the music industry."

While it is a blow to the recording industry, Friday's decision is unlikely to derail the RIAA's ongoing lawsuits against hundreds of individual file swappers. The ruling focuses on the unconventional subpoena power that the organization had claimed in order to seek ISP subscribers' identities and does not address the legality of the lawsuits that have already been filed.

File swappers are generally anonymous on peer-to-peer [P2P] networks, identified only by an Internet Protocol (IP) address assigned by their ISP. But names and addresses of subscribers can be determined by reviewing ISP records, which can connect IP addresses to individual accounts.

## File Swappers Will Be Sued

Even if the court's decision is ultimately upheld against appeals, the RIAA still will have the power to identify and sue file swappers.

The big difference, though, is this: The RIAA would have to file a "John Doe" lawsuit against each anonymous swapper, a process that would be considerably more labor-intensive and time-consuming. That in turn could limit the number of people the association has the resources to pursue.

"It is a pretty big setback," said Evan Cox, a copyright attorney with law firm Covington & Burling. "At the end of the day, it's a practical issue. It's mostly going to mean considerable extra expense and a fair amount of additional paperwork and formality."

The RIAA said it would continue its lawsuits against individual swappers, even if it is not able to use the subpoena power.

An RIAA executive said this new "John Doe" process would be more intrusive for individuals, not less, since the organization would no longer be able to contact potential lawsuit targets and settle before filing an official suit. For several months, it has been sending letters to suspected file-swappers after obtaining their identities from ISPs and offering a settlement instead of going to court.

"This decision is inconsistent with both the views of Congress and the findings of the district court," RIAA President Cary Sherman said in a statement. "It unfortunately means we can no longer notify illegal file sharers before we file lawsuits against them to offer the opportunity to settle outside of litigation. Verizon is solely responsible for a legal process that will now be less sensitive to the interests of its subscribers who engage in illegal activity."

The appeals court's decision comes after the RIAA sued 382 individuals alleged to have offered copyrighted music for download through file-swapping services such as Kazaa, and settled with 220 people for amounts averaging about $3,000 apiece. Many of those settlements had been made before suits were filed, the organization has said.

The suits have dramatically helped raise awareness of the legal issues surrounding file swapping and have also prompted considerable criticism—most notably after the group's first round of lawsuits targeted a 12-year-old honors student living in New York public housing. That suit was settled just a day after being filed, as the RIAA sought to defuse an immediate public relations backlash.

Most of the legal challenges to the RIAA's strategy have focused on the subpoena process used to obtain identities, rather than on the copyright lawsuits themselves.

## The DMCA Factor

Since the beginning of [2002], the RIAA has cited provisions in the Digital Millennium Copyright Act [DMCA] as the legal basis of its subpoena strategy. The subpoenas were used to get ISPs to reveal the identities of anonymous subscribers who, the RIAA alleged, were infringing copyrights by swapping files over peer-to-peer networks.

Unlike traditional subpoenas issued by law enforcement organizations, these were requested by a private group and were not attached to an ongoing lawsuit—factors that immediately drew criticism from civil rights groups.

Verizon, the first ISP to receive several such subpoenas, challenged them immediately, saying they were unconstitutional. A lower court ruled in favor of the RIAA earlier [in 2003], setting the stage for the hundreds of lawsuits it subsequently filed. SBC Communications, Charter Communications and the American Civil Liberties Union have also filed their own, separate challenges to the procedure.

Verizon welcomed [the] court decision, saying it would help protect the privacy of people on the Internet.

"Today's ruling is an important victory for Internet users and all consumers," Sarah Deutsch, a Verizon associate general counsel, said in a statement. "The court has knocked down a dangerous procedure that threatens Americans' traditional legal guarantees and violates their constitutional rights."

The appeals court did not talk about constitutionality or privacy in its decision Friday, but said only that Congress had not drafted the DMCA to apply to peer-to-peer networks.

The 1998 law came out of a bitter Congressional battle between copyright holders and telecommunications companies over liability for online infringement. The conflict ended in a compromise, which said that ISPs would not be held liable for communications that simply passed through their infrastructure, as opposed to stored on their servers or networks.

## No Application to P2P Networks

Using similar reasoning, the court said the law's subpoena provisions did not apply to peer-to-peer networks, since the copyrighted material was never stored on an ISP's network, but was transferred directly between users' computers.

"This certainly underscores what ISPs have said from the beginning," said Fred von Lohmann, an attorney for the Electronic Frontier Foundation, a civil liberties group that has been critical of the RIAA's strategy. "This was not the deal that was struck in the DMCA. Peer-to-peer [networks] did not exist when the DMCA was being drafted, and Congress did not have this kind of subpoena factory in mind."

The decision is likely to spark a new round of political skirmishing over copyright policy, although the RIAA did not say whether it would lobby Congress for a change in the law. Indeed, in its decision, the court said Congress may want to revisit the issue with the new technology in mind.

"The stakes are large for the music, motion picture, and software industries and their role in fostering technological innovation and our popular culture" the court wrote. "It is not surprising, therefore, that even as this case was being argued, committees of the Congress were considering how best to deal with the threat to copyrights posed by P2P file-sharing schemes."

"The court has, with this ruling, made it much harder for the RIAA to go after copyright infringers."

# The Court's Ruling Is a Major Setback in RIAA's Battle Against File Trading

*Pamela Jones*

*Pamela Jones is the editor of the noncommercial legal news site Groklaw. In the following viewpoint she discusses the federal appeals court's decision in RIAA v. Verizon and contends that it is extremely significant, as it has made it much more difficult and expensive to sue people suspected of illegally trading copyrighted files. RIAA had interpreted a provision of the Digital Millennium Copyright Act (DMCA) as enabling it to force Internet service providers (ISPs) to give them the names of users involved in peer-to-peer (P2P) file trading. However, Verizon's attorneys noticed something in the wording of the DMCA that had not been apparent before. The law did not authorize sending subpoenas without court authorization unless the ISP stored copyrighted files on its own servers, which in the case of P2P downloads does not occur. Jones praises Verizon's legal team for its analysis of the law and the judge for refusing to give in to RIAA's attempt to bend it.*

There was a case decided [in December 2003] by a federal appeals court, the U.S. Court of Appeals for the District of Columbia, that is so significant in its implications, at least to my reading, that I thought it worthwhile to explain it in detail. This is the second case I've seen now where someone tried to use the DMCA [Digital Millennium Copyright Act] for a purpose not intended by the legislators and in both cases it has now failed. Verizon brought a Motion to Quash [a subpoena] in the *RIAA v. Verizon* case, and the order [of the D.C. court] granted Verizon's motion.

If you click on Law.com ... and type in "quash" you will find out it just means "to annul or set aside. In law, a motion to quash asks the judge for an order setting aside or nullifying an action, such as 'quashing' service of a summons when the wrong person was served." In this case, it's a subpoena that is now quashed.

It isn't every day you read a judge write that a party's argument "borders upon the silly", but that is exactly how the judge here characterized one of the RIAA's arguments. In short, he wasn't even close to being persuaded, despite recognizing what he viewed as the seriousness of the situation faced by the RIAA in trying to stop file trading. . . .

The court has, with this ruling, made it much harder for the RIAA to go after copyright infringers. They can't just get a [law] clerk to sign a subpoena, send it to an ISP and get a subscriber's name, so they can go after the person. Because of this ruling, they'll have to take a different route, as I understand it, filling a "John Doe" case first, asking the court to tell them who the person is, which it may or may not agree to do. The RIAA will have to persuade the judge of two things: that they have a meritorious case and that they need to out the person instead of suing them as John Doe. If they succeed there on both prongs, then they can get the person's name and sue the alleged infringer by name.

It's far more expensive than a simple DMCA subpoena. Alternatively, they can try to pass a new law that gives them the powers they seek. According to Senator and songwriter Orrin Hatch, . . . there will be a push now in Congress to write a law that does what the RIAA wants. Still, it's more uphill for the RIAA now, and they are going to have to spend more time and money to take this to the next level. They can't just serve a clerk-issued subpoena on an ISP, get the names of infringers, threaten to sue and work out a deal with the terrified mothers of 12-year-old girls any more. There will be judicial oversight of the process. It's a major setback to the RIAA in its battle against file traders.

Those are the facts of the case and its implications, but the details are more interesting, to me, anyway, than the conflict between the RIAA and file sharers. Just as a programmer can find it very interesting to work on a challenging project for a boring company that makes the same widget all day long and nothing more stirring than that or even enjoy coding for a company he doesn't much like, so in the legal field the arguments are more interesting to those in the field than what the case happens to be about. Sometimes there is a dovetail of both. Making new law is what litigators live for. And Verizon just got a judge to fine-tune our understanding of the subpoena provisions of the DMCA's Section 512. Copyright law's landscape just experienced a bit of an earthquake.

The RIAA wanted Verizon to turn over the names of some of its customers who, the RIAA said, were illegally sharing music using P2P [peer-to-peer] software like Kazaa. Verizon didn't want to do that. They lost in a first scuffle in the lower court, but they bothered to take the time and trouble and spend the money to appeal. Some unknown, to me, attorney at Verizon ... had a legal brainstorm. It's the kind of brainstorm that changes the whole playing field. And whoever it is, I salute him or her or them. I also admire this court for the careful analysis given to the arguments and for understanding the brainstorm argument and accepting it.

## Judge Refused to Bend the Law

The impression I have formed is that some in the legal community have been viewing the DMCA as a handy "quick and dirty" way to get what they wanted for their clients, using the geek meaning of quick and dirty. It was quick, cheap and easy. And that is exactly what made it so likely to be abused, according to critics of the strategy. Verizon saw the issue in just those Constitutional, free speech terms, and more: "Verizon appealed, and company lawyer Sarah Deutsch called the ruling 'an important victory for all Internet users and all consumers. . . . Consumers' rights cannot be trampled upon in the quest to enforce your copyright,' Deutsch said."

Let me state that I don't personally download music, unless I have paid for it. I always try to keep the law, whatever it is, if only because it's my field, and that isn't the only reason. I believe in obeying laws, with the only exception being the kind that might get you prosecuted in a Nuremberg court [a court that tried Nazi war criminals] or before the Almighty for violations of his laws. That isn't something that usually comes up in the normal course of events, usually never in a person's lifetime. And this ruling isn't saying that the RIAA has no right to protect its copyright interests. But the DMCA and the way it was being used raised Constitutional questions in my mind. This judge, Chief Judge Douglas Ginsburg, although he seemed sympathetic to the RIAA's perceived problem with file traders, just couldn't see the DMCA as having been written to solve that particular problem. He refused to pretend that it did. And he refused to bend the law to suit the circumstances.

This is what I love so much about the law. You hear nasty lawyer jokes all the time, I know. So do I. And when there are decisions in a court that people don't like, it's not unusual to hear some cracks about the judge and the legal system. But my view is that these folks are what stand between us and chaos, between us and the bully process, whereby special interests grab whatever they want at the expense of everyone else, based on money and power. The parties naturally fight for what they perceive to be in their best interest. But judges are supposed to look at the bigger picture and to consider the impact on the general public as well. Frankly, they sometimes seem to be the last ones in the scheme of things still reliably looking at anything but the bottom line. Decisions are sometimes disappointing, but now and then, a judge stands up and says: we have a rule of law here, and no matter who you are, no matter how much money you have, no matter how powerful your friends are, here in my courtroom, the law is applied fairly and without partiality. When you see it happen, it's a beautiful sight.

Judges don't do what they do for the money. They make an OK living, but there are easier ways to make money, lots more money than a judge will ever see, if he or she is honest. They do it because they love the law and the protections it is meant to provide to everyone; they love finding the balance, the attempt to decide fairness, the interplay between private interests and Constitutional guarantees, the opportunity to figure out what the framers of the Constitution and the lesser laws had in mind in the first place. The US legal system is based on the fundamental principle that when you go to court, it ought to actually be justice that you get. There has always been an idealism built into the country's judicial branch that moves my heart.

Judges are supposed to be the implementers and real-world fine-tuners of the decisions the legislators make. In this case, that is exactly what happened. A judge would have liked to rule differently, probably, all things being equal, but he noticed a detail in the DMCA, thanks to Verizon's brilliant attorney(s) and his own reading of the legislators' stated intent, and he couldn't get around what he saw. That is the rule of law, where you accept what it says, regardless of personal feelings, out of respect for the process.

## Verizon's Legal Team Thought Well

And one other thing: if there is one thing people invariably resent, it's paying legal fees. But bear in mind that you are paying someone to think creatively for you, and that does take time. You can't do a good job without taking the time to research and really think things through in great detail. The more you pay your lawyer, the more he will do that for you. The less you are willing to pay, the less time he or she will be able to devote to that very necessary part of the whole. What you are paying for is not only their prior knowledge of the law, not just to have them show up in court for you. You are paying them to think about the law and how it applies to *your* situation. It takes time to do that well.

Here, Verizon's legal team thought very well indeed. It takes time and a background in a particular field to know what might make a difference in a case, and then it takes courage to put the idea forward, particularly if it's a new idea that has never prevailed in a case before, maybe never even been tried before. They did exactly that, and despite amicus briefs [written legal arguments submitted to a court by nonlitigants in a case] by the US and the Department of Justice, Verizon won. If I had come up with the arguments Verizon put forward, I'd be happy for the rest of my life just thinking about it and remembering it and bragging to my grandkids someday about it. Let's take a look at the ruling. . . .

Section 512(h) is the section of the DMCA that makes it possible to serve subpoenas on ISPs to force them to disclose the names of internet users. . . . Here is the exact language of the DMCA's Section 512(h):

"(h) Subpoena To Identify Infringer.

"(1) Request.—"A copyright owner or a person authorized to act on the owner's behalf may request the clerk of any United States district court to issue a subpoena to a service provider for identification of an alleged infringer in accordance with this subsection." . . .

"(4) Basis for granting subpoena.—If the notification filed satisfies the provisions of subsection (c)(3)(A), the proposed subpoena is in proper form, and the accompanying declaration is properly executed, the clerk shall expeditiously issue and sign the proposed subpoena and return it to the requester for delivery to the service provider.

"(5) Actions of service provider receiving subpoena.—Upon receipt of the issued subpoena, either accompanying or subsequent to the receipt of a notification described in subsection (c)(3)(A), the service provider shall expeditiously disclose to the copyright owner or person authorized by the copyright owner the information required by the subpoena, notwithstanding any other provision of law and regardless of whether the service provider responds to the notification." . . .

This, then, is what looked so simple and appealing to the RIAA. No need to even ask a judge's permission to obtain the subpoena. Just file with the court, and presto! you are in business. The ISP has no choice but to comply. Or so they thought. But Verizon said, Wait just a minute, here. We are an ISP. In the case of file traders, with Kazaa and that type of file trading arrangement, there is nothing stored by us. We provide internet access only. We can't be in the business of regulating what people do with their own computers, just as we can't be responsible for what they say in email, which we merely transmit. The RIAA said, Oh, your honor, this Section 512 is part of the entire Section and we have the right to demand that they just hand over the names and we'll do the rest.

Verizon noticed a detail that had escaped notice before. Section 512(h), they argued, does not authorize the issuance of a subpoena to an ISP that merely transmits infringing material but does not store it on its servers. The RIAA argued Section 512(h) authorizes the issuance of a subpoena without regard to whether the ISP is acting as a conduit for user-directed communications. The judge decided from both the terms of Section 512(h) and the overall structure of Section 512(h) that, "as Verizon contends, a subpoena may be issued only to an ISP engaged in storing on its servers material that is infringing or the subject of infringing activity."

If you take the time to follow the judge through the details of his decision, you'll see why I love the law so much and find it so endlessly intriguing.

# CHAPTER 2

# The Counterhacking of a Computer to Protect a Network Is Constitutional

# Case Overview

## United States v. Heckenkamp (2007)

Jerome Heckenkamp was a talented hacker—a white-hat hacker (that is, not a malicious one), he initially claimed. A brilliant computer security expert who graduated from college at the age of eighteen, he had become a network engineer at Los Alamos National Laboratories in New Mexico. But he lost his job in 2001 when prosecutors charged him with having defaced eBay's Web site in 1999, while he was a graduate student at the University of Wisconsin. After several years of court proceedings, at one point during which he fired his attorney and insisted on representing himself in court, Heckenkamp pleaded guilty to a series of cybercrimes, including the installation of trojan horse (hidden malicious) programs not only on eBay computers but on those of Qualcomm and a number of other companies. In 2005 he was sentenced to eight months in prison in addition to time already served, followed by eight months of home confinement with electronic monitoring and another three years of supervised release.

But that outcome is not the most significant aspect of the case. Earlier, Heckenkamp had tried to get evidence suppressed on grounds that the remote search of the computer in his University of Wisconsin dorm room was unconstitutional, a motion that had been denied. At the time he pleaded guilty, he reserved the right for his attorney to appeal the denial, and so in 2007 a U.S. court of appeals considered the question of whether the search violated his constitutional rights. Normally, a search requires a warrant issued by a judge. If authorities conduct a search without one, the evidence obtained from it cannot be used in court; this is called the "exclusionary rule." But there are a few exceptions to the rule. The question before the court was whether the search in Heckenkamp's case came under the "special needs" exception, and the court's ruling would set a precedent for other cases in the future.

The search was conducted by University of Wisconsin network administrator Jeffrey Savoy at the request of Qualcomm, which had traced unauthorized system access to the university. Savoy discovered that someone in a dorm room had gained unauthorized access both to Qualcomm's computers and to a university mail server. He found evidence that Heckenkamp's computer had been the one used and reported this to the FBI, which was investigating the Qualcomm case. The FBI agent told him that he would get a warrant to search the computer. But that night, Savoy began to worry about the security of the university's mail server. He had blocked the intruder's access to it, but he knew that a hacker could change a computer's identification and might want to disrupt the university's mail system. So he logged on from home and hacked into the intruder's computer himself, finding that its IP (Internet protocol) address had indeed been changed. He did not delete or modify any files, but after contacting the FBI again and learning that no search warrant had yet been obtained, he went with the university police to Heckenkamp's room and physically disconnected the computer from the network.

Was Savoy's warrantless remote search of the computer legal? The court decided that it was, because he had acted not to obtain evidence against Heckenkamp, but to protect the university's mail server. People do have a right to expect privacy on their computers, even computers attached to networks, the court said—and this is an important principle that had not been legally established before—but when special needs, apart from the normal need for law enforcement, make obtaining a warrant impractical, searching without a warrant is justifiable, the court ruled.

"Although Heckenkamp had a reasonable expectation of privacy in his personal computer, a limited warrantless
remote search of the computer was justified under the special needs exception."

# The Court's Opinion: Exceptions to the Right to Privacy Regarding Personal Computers Are Allowed

*Sidney Thomas*

*Sidney Thomas has been a judge of the U.S. Court of Appeals
for the Ninth Circuit since 1996 and is considered one of its
most liberal members. In the following opinion in* United States
v. Heckenkamp, *he relates in detail how and why a University
of Wisconsin computer network administrator remotely searched
graduate student Jerome Heckenkamp's computer without a warrant. The administrator acted only to protect the network from
being hacked, Thomas says, and not to gather evidence against
Heckenkamp, even though the administrator turned the evidence
over to the FBI. Therefore, the search was covered by an exception to the Fourth Amendment rule requiring search warrants.
Although individuals do have a right to expect that the content
of their computers will be private, Heckenkamp had assented to
university policies when he connected his computer to its network, and those policies authorized limited security measures.*

Sidney Thomas, opinion, *United States v. Heckenkamp*, U.S. Court of Appeals for the
Ninth Circuit, April 6, 2007. Reproduced by permission.

*Therefore, the court of appeals ruled that the lower court was right to deny his motion to suppress the evidence of his criminal activity as having been illegally obtained.*

In this case, we consider whether a remote search of computer files on a hard drive by a network administrator was justified under the "special needs" exception to the Fourth Amendment because the administrator reasonably believed the computer had been used to gain unauthorized access to confidential records on a university computer. We conclude that the remote search was justified. . . .

In December 1999, Scott Kennedy, a computer system administrator for Qualcomm Corporation in San Diego, California, discovered that somebody had obtained unauthorized access to (or "hacked into," in popular parlance) the company's computer network. Kennedy contacted Special Agent Terry Rankhorn of the Federal Bureau of Investigation about the intrusion.

Kennedy was able to trace the intrusion to a computer on the University of Wisconsin at Madison network, and he contacted the university's computer help desk, seeking assistance. Jeffrey Savoy, the University of Wisconsin computer network investigator, promptly responded to Kennedy's request and began examining the university's system. Savoy found evidence that someone using a computer on the university network was in fact hacking into the Qualcomm system and that the user had gained unauthorized access to the university's system as well. Savoy was particularly concerned that the user had gained access to the "Mail2" server on the university system, which housed accounts for 60,000 individuals on campus and processed approximately 250,000 emails each day. At that time, students on campus were preparing for final exams, and Savoy testified that "the disruption on campus would be tremendous if e-mail was destroyed." Through his investigation of the Mail2 server, Savoy traced the source of intrusion to a computer located in university housing. The type of access the user had obtained was restricted to specific system administrators, none of whom would be working from the university's dormitories.

Savoy determined that the computer that had gained unauthorized access had a university Internet Protocol ("IP") address that ended in 117. In addition, Savoy determined that Heckencamp, who was a computer science graduate student at the university, had checked his email from that IP address 20 minutes before and 40 minutes after the unauthorized connections between the computer at the IP address ending in 117, the Mail2 server, and the Qualcomm server. Savoy determined that the computer at that IP address had been used regularly to check Heckencamp's email account, but no others. Savoy became extremely concerned because he knew that Heckenkamp had been terminated from his job at the university computer help desk two years earlier for similar unauthorized activity, and Savoy knew that Heckenkamp "had technical expertise to damage [the university's] system."

## Action Taken to Protect Mail Server

Although Savoy was confident that the computer that had gained the unauthorized access belonged to Heckenkamp, he checked the housing records to ensure that the IP address was assigned to Heckenkamp's dorm room. The housing department initially stated that the IP address corresponded to a different room down the hall from Heckenkamp's assigned room. The housing department acknowledged that the records could be inaccurate but stated that they would not be able to verify the location of the IP address until the next morning. In order to protect the university's server, Savoy electronically blocked the connection between IP address 117 and the Mail2 server.

After blocking the connection, Savoy contacted Rankhorn. After Savoy informed Rankhorn of the information he had found, Rankhorn told Savoy that he intended to get a warrant for the computer, but he did not ask Savoy to take any action or to commence any investigation.

Later that night, Savoy decided to check the status of the 117 computer from home because he was still concerned about the integrity of the university's system. He logged into the network and determined that the 117 computer was not attached to the network. However, Savoy was still concerned that the same computer could have "changed its identity," so he checked the networking hardware to determine if the computer that was originally logged on at the 117 address was now logged on at a different IP address. His search confirmed that the computer was now logged on at an IP address ending in 120.

Based on this discovery, Savoy became even more concerned that the Mail2 server "security could be compromised at any time," particularly because "the intruder at this point knows that he's being investigated" and might therefore interfere with the system to cover his tracks. Savoy concluded that he needed to act that night.

Before taking action, Savoy wanted to verify that the computer logged on at 120 was the same computer that had been logged on at 117 earlier in the day. He logged into the computer, using a name and password he had discovered in his earlier investigation into the 117 computer. Savoy used a series of commands to confirm that the 120 computer was the same computer that had been logged on at 117 and to determine whether the computer still posed a risk to the university server. After approximately 15 minutes of looking only in the temporary directory, without deleting, modifying, or destroying any files, Savoy logged off of the computer.

Savoy then determined that "[the 120] machine need[ed] to get off line immediately or as soon as possible" based on "a university security need." He contacted both Rankhorn and a Detective Scheller, who worked for the university police. Savoy informed them of his discoveries and concerns. Rankhorn asked Savoy to wait to take action because he was attempting to get a search warrant. However, Savoy felt that he needed to protect the university's system by taking the machine off line immediately. Therefore, he made the decision to coordinate with the university police to take the computer off line and to "let [the] university police coordinate with the FBI."

## Heckenkamp Caught

Together with Scheller and other university police officers, Savoy went to the room assigned to Heckenkamp. When they arrived at the room, the door was ajar, and nobody was in the room. Savoy and Scheller entered the room and disconnected the network cord attaching the computer to the network. Savoy noted that the computer had a screen saver with a password, which prevented him from accessing the computer. In order to be sure that the computer he had disconnected from the network was the computer that had gained unauthorized access to the Mail2 server, Savoy wanted to run some commands on the computer. Detective Scheller located Heckenkamp, explained the situation and asked for Heckenkamp's password, which Heckenkamp voluntarily provided.

Savoy used the password to run the commands on the computer and verified that it was the computer used to gain the unauthorized access. After Savoy confirmed that he had the right computer, Scheller advised Heckenkamp that he was not under arrest, but Scheller requested that Heckenkamp waive his Miranda rights [the right to remain silent] and give a statement. Heckenkamp waived his rights in writing and answered the investigator's and detectives' questions. In addition, Heckenkamp authorized Savoy to make a copy of his hard drive for later analysis, which Savoy did. At no time did Savoy or Scheller search Heckenkamp's room. Throughout his testimony, Savoy emphasized that his actions were taken to protect the university's server rather than for law enforcement purposes.

The federal agents obtained a search warrant from the Western District of Wisconsin, which was executed the following day. Pursuant to the warrant, the agents seized the computer and searched Heckenkamp's room.

Heckenkamp was indicted in both the Northern and Southern Districts of California on multiple offenses, including counts of recklessly causing damage by intentionally accessing a protected computer without authorization.... In separate orders, Judge Ware in the Northern District and Judge Jones in the Southern District denied Heckenkamp's motions to suppress the evidence gathered from (1) the remote search of his computer, (2) the image taken of his computer's hard drive, and (3) the search conducted pursuant to the FBI's search warrant.

The two cases were eventually consolidated before Judge Ware. Heckenkamp entered a conditional guilty plea to two counts ... which allowed him to appeal the denials of his motions to suppress....

## Right to Computer Privacy

As a prerequisite to establishing the illegality of a search under the Fourth Amendment, a defendant must show that he had a reasonable expectation of privacy in the place searched. An individual has a reasonable expectation of privacy if he can "'demonstrate a subjective expectation that his activities would be private, and he [can] show that his expectation was one that society is prepared to recognize as reasonable.'" *United States v. Bautista.* No single factor determines whether an individual legitimately may claim under the Fourth Amendment that a place should be free of warrantless government intrusion. However, we have given weight to such factors as the defendant's possessory interest in the property searched or seized, the measures taken by the defendant to insure privacy, whether the materials are in a container labeled as being private, and the presence or absence of a right to exclude others from access.

The government does not dispute that Heckenkamp had a subjective expectation of privacy in his computer and his dormitory room, and there is no doubt that Heckenkamp's subjective expectation as to the latter was legitimate and objectively reasonable. We hold that he also had a legitimate, objectively reasonable expectation of privacy in his personal computer.

The salient question is whether the defendant's objectively reasonable expectation of privacy in his computer was eliminated when he attached it to the university network. We conclude under the facts of this case that the act of attaching his computer to the network did not extinguish his legitimate, objectively reasonable privacy expectations.

A person's reasonable expectation of privacy may be diminished in "transmissions over the Internet or e-mail that have already arrived at the recipient." *United States v. Lifshitz.* However, the mere act of accessing a network does not in itself extinguish privacy expectations, nor does the fact that others may have occasional access to the computer. However, privacy expectations may be reduced if the user is advised that information transmitted through the network is not confidential and that the systems administrators may monitor communications transmitted by the user.

In the instant [present] case, there was no announced monitoring policy on the network. To the contrary, the university's computer policy itself provides that "[i]n general, all computer and electronic files should be free from access by any but the authorized users of those files. Exceptions to this basic principle shall be kept to a minimum and made only where essential to . . . protect the integrity of the University and the rights and property of the state." When examined in their entirety, university policies do not eliminate Heckenkamp's expectation of privacy in his computer. Rather, they establish limited instances in which university administrators may access his computer in order to protect the university's systems. Therefore, we must reject the government's contention that Heckenkamp had no objectively reasonable expectation of privacy in his personal computer, which was protected by a screensaver password, located in his dormitory room, and subject to no policy allowing the university actively to monitor or audit his computer usage.

## Computer Search Justified

Although we conclude that Heckenkamp had a reasonable expectation of privacy in his personal computer, we conclude that the search of the computer was justified under the "special needs" exception to the warrant requirement. Under the special needs exception, a warrant is not required when "'special needs, beyond the normal need for law enforcement, make the warrant and probable-cause requirement impracticable.'" *Griffin v. Wisconsin*. If a court determines that such conditions exist, it will "assess the constitutionality of the search by balancing the need to search against the intrusiveness of the search." *Henderson v. City of Simi Valley*.

Here, Savoy provided extensive testimony that he was acting to secure the Mail2 server, and that his actions were not motivated by a need to collect evidence for law enforcement purposes or at the request of law enforcement agents. This undisputed evidence supports Judge Jones's conclusion that the special needs exception applied. The integrity and security of the campus e-mail system was in jeopardy. Although Savoy was aware that the FBI was also investigating the use of a computer on the university network to hack into the Qualcomm system, his actions were not taken for law enforcement purposes. Not only is there no evidence that Savoy was acting at the behest of law enforcement, but also the record indicates that Savoy was acting contrary to law enforcement requests that he delay action.

Under these circumstances, a search warrant was not necessary because Savoy was acting purely within the scope of his role as a system administrator. Under the university's policies, to which Heckenkamp assented when he connected his computer to the university's network, Savoy was authorized to "rectif[y] emergency situations that threaten the integrity of campus computer or communication systems[,] provided that use of accessed files is limited solely to maintaining or safeguarding the system." Savoy discovered through his examination of the network logs, in which Heckenkamp had no reasonable expectation of privacy, that the computer that he had earlier blocked from the network was now operating from a different IP address, which itself was a violation of the university's network policies.

This discovery, together with Savoy's earlier discovery that the computer had gained root access to the university's Mail2 server, created a situation in which Savoy needed to act immediately to protect the system. Although he was aware that the FBI was already seeking a warrant to search Heckenkamp's computer in order to serve the FBI's law enforcement needs, Savoy believed that the university's separate security interests required immediate action. Just as requiring a warrant to investigate potential student drug use would disrupt operation of a high school, requiring a warrant to investigate potential misuse of the university's computer network would disrupt the operation of the university and the network that it relies upon in order to function. Moreover, Savoy and the other network administrators generally do not have the same type of "adversarial relationship" with the university's network users as law enforcement officers generally have with criminal suspects.

The district court was entirely correct in holding that the special needs exception applied.

## Motion to Suppress Evidence Denied

Once a court determines that the special needs doctrine applies to a search, it must "assess the constitutionality of the search by balancing the need to search against the intrusiveness of the search." *Henderson*. The factors considered are the subject of the search's privacy interest, the government's interests in performing the search, and the scope of the intrusion.

Here, although Heckenkamp had a subjectively real and objectively reasonable expectation of privacy in his computer, the university's interest in maintaining the security of its network provided a compelling government interest in determining the source of the unauthorized intrusion into sensitive files. The remote search of the computer was remarkably limited given the circumstances. Savoy did not view, delete, or modify any of the actual files on the computer; he was only logged into the computer for 15 minutes; and he sought only to verify that the same computer that had been connected at the 117 IP address was now connected at the 120 IP address. Here, as in *Henderson*, "the government interest served[] and the relative unobtrusiveness of the search" lead to a conclusion that the remote search was not unconstitutional.

The district court did not err in denying the motion to suppress the evidence obtained through the remote search of the computer.

The district court also did not err in denying the motion to suppress evidence obtained during the searches of Heckenkamp's room. Assuming, without deciding, that Savoy and the university police violated Heckenkamp's Fourth Amendment rights when they entered his dormitory room for non-law-enforcement purposes, the evidence obtained through the search was nonetheless admissible under the independent source exception to the exclusionary rule.

Under the independent source exception, "'information which is received through an illegal source is considered to be cleanly obtained when it arrives through an independent source.'" *Murray v. United States.* . . . In order to determine whether evidence obtained through a tainted warrant is admissible, "[a] reviewing court should excise the tainted evidence and determine whether the remaining untainted evidence would provide a neutral magistrate with probable cause to issue a warrant."

Here, even without the evidence gathered through the allegedly improper search, there is sufficient information in the affidavit to establish probable cause. The affidavit recited evidence that the server intrusion had been tracked "to a campus dormitory room computer belonging to Jerome T. Heckenkamp"; that "[t]he computer is in Room 107, Noyes House, Adams Hall on the University of Wisconsin-Madison"; and that "Heckenkamp previously had a disciplinary action in the past for unauthorized computer access to a University of Wisconsin system." This was sufficient evidence to obtain the warrant to search "Room 107, Noyes House, Adams Hall."

Although Heckenkamp had a reasonable expectation of privacy in his personal computer, a limited warrantless remote search of the computer was justified under the special needs exception to the warrant requirement. The subsequent search of his dorm room was justified, based on information obtained by means independent of the university search of the room. Therefore, the district courts properly denied the suppression motions.

> "[Heckenkamp] *may also impact the electronic privacy of persons whose computers are attached to certain networks, both in academia, and elsewhere, including persons who have committed no crimes."*

# The *Heckenkamp* Ruling May Affect the Privacy of Innocent Citizens

*David Carney*

*David Carney is an attorney who writes and publishes* Tech Law Journal, *an online publication offering news and analysis of legislation and litigation affecting computer and communications technology. In the following report he presents the background of* United States v. Heckenkamp *and explains the basis of the court of appeals' decision. First, he notes, the court determined that Jerome Heckencamp did have a reasonable expectation of privacy on his computer; however, it then ruled that it was legal for university officials to search its hard drive without a warrant because there is an exception to the rule that search warrants are necessary; they are not required when "special needs, beyond the normal need for law enforcement" make obtaining a warrant impractical. In this case, the university was motivated not by a desire to assist the FBI in its investigation of Jerome Heckenkamp's alleged crimes, but by a concern that its computer network was threatened by hacking. The ruling, Carney argues, may affect many people, even those who have not committed crimes, because knowing that evidence obtained without a war-*

David Carney, "9th Circuit Constrains Computer Privacy," *Tech Law Journal*, April 6, 2007. Reproduced by permission.

*rant need not always be suppressed will reduce the incentive for investigators to respect network users' privacy.*

April 6, 2007. The U.S. Court of Appeals (9thCir) issued its opinion in *USA v. Heckenkamp*, a Section 1030 case in which the issue is the admissibility of evidence acquired in a warrantless remote search of a student's hard drive by a university network administrator who was acting in association with the FBI.

The Court of Appeals affirmed the District Court's denial of Heckenkamp's motion to suppress evidence under the special needs exception to the warrant requirement. The Court of Appeals held that federal prosecutors can use evidence collected in a warrantless computer search to prosecute a student for hacking computers outside of the university network, when the university acted out of an independent concern to protect its own computer systems.

Background. The Federal Bureau of Investigation (FBI) was investigating unauthorized access to the computer systems of Qualcomm. It determined that the intruder likely accessed Qualcomm's computer systems from a computer on the University of Wisconsin (UW) network.

The FBI then sought and received assistance from the UW. A UW investigation of network information led it to focus on one individual, Jerome Heckenkamp, who was a graduate student in computer science, and the computer in his UW dormitory room. The UW investigation determined that a computer, or two computers, it was not sure, under investigation, may have been used to gain unauthorized access to both Qualcomm's computer system and the UW e-mail system.

At this point, neither the FBI, nor UW police, had obtained a search warrant, or permission from Heckenkamp, to search his computer. Nevertheless, a UW network administrator used his computer to remotely search the hard drive of Heckenkamp's computer.

The next day the FBI obtained the first search warrant. Pursuant to the warrant, federal agents seized Heckenkamp's computer and searched his room.

Heckenkamp moved to suppress evidence gathered from the UW's remote search of his computer, an image taken of his hard drive, and the search conducted pursuant to the FBI's search warrant. The District Court denied the motion.

Heckenkamp pled guilty to two counts of violation of 18 U.S.C. § 1030, conditioned upon his right to appeal the denial of his motion to suppress. Heckenkamp then brought the present appeals.

Court of Appeals. The Court of Appeals affirmed. Heckenkamp prevailed on the issue of whether he held a reasonable expectation of privacy in the contents of his computer. The Court of Appeals opinion provides guidance regarding when there is a reasonable expectation of privacy in computers that are attached to networks. However, Heckenkamp lost on the second issue—the special needs exception to the warrant and probable cause requirement.

The Court of Appeals first addressed the warrant requirement and reasonable expectations of privacy. It wrote that "As a prerequisite to establishing the illegality of a search under the Fourth Amendment, a defendant must show that he had a reasonable expectation of privacy in the place searched."

The Court also noted that the "government does not dispute that Heckenkamp had a subjective expectation of privacy in his computer and his dormitory room, and there is no doubt that Heckenkamp's subjective expectation as to the latter was legitimate and objectively reasonable." However, it wrote that the "salient question is whether the defendant's objectively reasonable expectation of privacy in his computer was eliminated when he attached it to the university network. We conclude under the facts of this case that the act of attaching his computer to the network did not extinguish his legitimate, objectively reasonable privacy expectations."

The Court added that "privacy expectations may be reduced if the user is advised that information transmitted through the network is not confidential and that the systems administrators may monitor communications transmitted by the user." But, "In the instant [present] case, there was no announced monitoring policy on the network." After reviewing the UW's policies, the Court concluded that "we must reject the government's contention that Heckenkamp had no objectively reasonable expectation of privacy in his personal computer, which was protected by a screensaver password, located in his dormitory room, and subject to no policy allowing the university actively to monitor or audit his computer usage."

The Court of Appeals then addressed the second issue, the special needs exception. It concluded that "the search of the computer was justified under the 'special needs' exception to the warrant requirement. Under the special needs exception, a warrant is not required when 'special needs, beyond the normal need for law enforcement, make the warrant and probable-cause requirement impracticable.'"

The Court of Appeals wrote that while the UW knew of the FBI investigation regarding unauthorized access to Qualcomm's computer, it had an independent concern about the security of its own computers. Moreover, this concern about its own computers was enough to allow it to rush the investigation without a warrant.

The evidence collected by the warrantless search of the computer was used to obtain the conviction in the FBI's case. Nevertheless, the Court of Appeals wrote that the actions of the UW investigator "were not motivated by a need to collect evidence for law enforcement purposes or at the request of law enforcement agents."

Hence, the Court of Appeals affirmed the denial of the motion to suppress under this special needs exception to the warrant requirement.

Commentary. Heckenkamp pled guilty to hacking into Qualcomm's computer system. His conviction has withstood appeal, and he will be punished. Suppression of evidence in this case may have enabled Heckenkamp to escape punishment for a crime to which he pled guilty.

However, this opinion may also impact the electronic privacy of persons whose computers are attached to certain networks, both in academia, and elsewhere, including persons who have committed no crimes.

The exclusionary rule can wreak havoc on a prosecution. Occasionally, it enables guilty people to escape punishment. Law enforcement officials and prosecutors hate it when this happens.

Courts and legislators have only limited means by which they can incent overzealous prosecutors and investigators to respect the constitutional privacy rights of the general public. The exclusionary rule can be an effective tool. The loosening of the exclusionary rule in this case removes some of the incentive for prosecutors and investigators, including university police, to respect the privacy of users of their networks.

Also, in the present case, the Court of Appeals noted that the UW investigators had reason to suspect that a computer or computers that may have been used by Heckenkamp had accessed the university's e-mail system without authorization. The Court relied on this in finding that the special needs exception applied in this case.

However, the opinion does not provide clear guidance for related factual scenarios. For example, can a university network administrator remotely search a user's computer without a warrant under the special needs exception solely on the basis that the FBI has asserted that a user of the university network has hacked an outside computer system[?]

Moreover, the opinion is silent as to investigations by corporations, trade groups, or other non-law enforcement entities. Finally, the opinion does not address application of the special needs exemption in the context of online criminal activity other than Section 1030 unauthorized access.

> "*[The system administrator] may have been acting to protect the university, but he was also investigating the offense. That should have made his warrantless search unconstitutional.*"

# The Warrantless Search of the Accused Hacker's Computer Was Unconstitutional

*Jennifer Granick*

*Jennifer Granick is executive director of the Stanford Law School Center for Internet and Society. She was Jerome Heckencamp's attorney for a while after he was first arrested. In the following viewpoint she talks about his case,* United States. v. Heckencamp, *and argues that the University of Wisconsin's search of his computer without a warrant violated the Fourth Amendment. She says that the Court of Appeals was right to affirm that people have an expectation of privacy in the information stored on their computers, but wrong to endorse a "special needs" exception to the rule that a warrant must be obtained if the government performs a search. The university claimed that it had to search immediately to protect its network from hacking, but, Granick contends, the fact remains that the man who did the searching was suspicious of Heckencamp and intended all along to give the results to law enforcement officers. She points out that many searches in response to computer security breaches have*

Jennifer Granick, "Appeals Court Misfired in Hack-Counterhack Dispute," *Wired.com*, April 11, 2007. Copyright © 2008 Condé Nast Publications. All rights reserved. Originally published by *Wired.com* Reprinted by permission.

*the purpose of making a case against the intruder in addition to fixing the breach, and that future prosecutors will try to take advantage of the Court's ruling in this case.*

Last week's decision [in April 2007] by the U.S. 9th Circuit Court of Appeals in *U.S. v. Heckenkamp* is a mixed bag. It assures us that a college student's dorm room computer is protected by the Fourth Amendment but says warrantless, and perhaps even suspicionless, searches of those computers can be justified by a university's "special needs."

It's great that the court rejected the government's view that we have no expectation of privacy in information stored on the hard drives of a computer we connect to school or other networks. But how much protection do we really have from random searches if the special-needs exception applies?

I especially care about this decision because I represented the defendant, Jerome Heckenkamp, early in the case. The charges involved allegations of hacking into Qualcomm and a host of other computer companies, as well as defacing eBay's webpage.

Heckenkamp was young and smart, but naïve; he'd been home schooled, was the apple of his parents' eye, and attended college close to where he grew up, at the University of Wisconsin. Upon graduation, he got a job at Los Alamos National Laboratory and moved away from his home state. He lost that job when FBI agents came to arrest him one morning in January of 2001. The family hired me to represent him.

In time, our attorney-client relationship frayed. Heckenkamp fired me and represented himself for approximately eight months—months he spent sitting in jail without any scheduled court dates, following a hearing in which he argued that the indictment against him should be dismissed because it spelled his name all in capital letters. Eventually, Heckenkamp hired San Diego–based attorney Benjamin Coleman to represent him.

## Search of Heckenkamp's Computer

One of the primary issues for both me and attorney Coleman centered on the legality of a remote search that the university system administrator conducted of Heckenkamp's dorm-room computer.

FBI and Qualcomm investigators were able to trace the Qualcomm intrusion through several hops to the "Mail2" e-mail server at the University of Wisconsin. At their direction, system administrator Jeffrey Savoy located a strange file on the mail server listing numerous logins to other computers through Mail2. The file also showed that someone had accessed a student dorm computer with an IP address ending in 117 using an account with the username and password "temp."

Savoy drew the conclusion (which proved correct) that the 117 computer was the source of the unauthorized access to Mail2. Savoy then looked at the e-mail-server logs and found IP address 117 checking the e-mail account for Heckenkamp, which led him to believe that 117 was assigned to Heckenkamp's machine. He blocked that IP from connecting to Mail2 and informed the investigating FBI agent. Savoy then went home.

That night, Savoy got to thinking about the events of the day. He logged on from home to determine what the 117 computer was up to—it was not online. But Savoy crosschecked the log of Ethernet addresses with IP addresses, and found the computer formerly known at 117 was now known as 120.

Savoy gave several plausible and not-inconsistent reasons for doing what he did next, the evening of December 8, 1999. He wanted to protect the mail system from a potentially destructive intruder; he wanted to find out who had been accessing Mail2; he wanted to confirm that the 117 computer was the same machine now using 120. He wanted to confirm that Heckenkamp was involved.

Whatever his motivation, Savoy logged on to the 120 machine using the "temp/temp" username and password he had found on Mail2. He spent 15 minutes there, looking at a phonebook file, and a list of account names, and found information that led him to believe Heckenkamp had an account on the machine. He also saw what he called "computer hacking tools" and files that Qualcomm had described. Savoy made screen-print copies of these files as evidence.

Savoy then decided to get the computer offline ASAP, informed the FBI and university police and, despite the FBI asking him to wait for a warrant, went to Heckenkamp's dorm room to disconnect the machine and secure the premises.

School police went to Heckenkamp's room and unplugged his machine from the network late that same night. FBI agents showed up with a warrant late on December 9th. The warrant affidavit failed to mention that Savoy had remotely searched the computer, and had searched Heckenkamp's dorm room without a warrant, though the agents were aware of both. The warrant simply said Savoy had tracked the intrusion to Heckenkamp's dorm-room computer.

I argued in court that the warrantless search was improper, as did Coleman later. We lost. Heckenkamp went on to plead guilty for time served, but retained the right to appeal his motion to suppress.

## Appeals Court's Decision

Last week's appeals court opinion starts out pretty well for computer privacy—the University of Wisconsin is a state school, so the Fourth Amendment, which only covers state action, applies to its activities. The court rejected a government assertion that students don't have privacy rights in their personal computers that they connect to a dorm or university network. That part of the ruling is a relief—imagine if connecting your computer to any private network meant police could search your system remotely without cause or authorization.

The court even held that the fact that others may have occasional access to a computer, does not diminish the owner's reasonable expectation of privacy in its contents—countering a few often-cited cases holding that disclosure of personal information to third parties destroys constitutional protections.

But then the court nonetheless upheld the remote, warrantless search of Heckenkamp's computer under the "special needs" exception to the Fourth Amendment.

That exception was carved out in a 1985 U.S. Supreme Court decision in *New Jersey v. T.L.O.*, a case in which a high school principal searched a student's purse. The court found that the public interest was best served by lowering the level of suspicion needed for a school search from "probable cause" to one of mere "reasonableness", and doing away with any warrant requirement.

Justice [Harry] Blackmun's concurrence limited the seemingly broad ruling to those exceptional circumstances in which "special needs", beyond the normal need for law enforcement, make the warrant and probable-cause requirement impractical. In subsequent cases, the high court has applied the special needs exception to a search of a doctor's office for administrative disciplinary proceedings, to probation searches, to drug testing following train accidents and prior to promotion to certain positions in the U.S. customs agency.

The Supreme Court has rejected the special needs exception for suspicionless blanket drug testing of candidates for public office. It also rejected it where a hospital initiated a program of drug testing pregnant women and disclosing the information to prosecutors.

In *Heckenkamp*, the 9th Circuit found that the special needs exception applied because Savoy remotely searched Heckenkamp's computer for the purpose of securing the Mail2 server, and not with a motivation to collect evidence for law enforcement purposes. The court then balanced the need to search against the intrusiveness of the search, and ruled that what Savoy did was permissible.

The application of "special needs" here is pretty narrow, and tied closely to the facts of this case. The court, for example, took into account that Savoy did not delete or modify any of the files on Heckenkamp's computer; was logged into the machine for only 15 minutes; and sought only to verify that the same computer that had been connected at 117 was now using 120.

## Why the Court Was Mistaken

Still, I think the 9th Circuit got it wrong. Remember, Savoy's search began after he discovered that someone using the university's Mail2 server had logged into Heckenkamp's machine. The 9th Circuit classifies this as evidence that Heckenkamp's computer was the source of the hack. But as far as Savoy knew, Mail2 compromised Heckenkamp's computer, not the other way around. Only the remote search produced evidence to the contrary.

Additionally, Savoy had other reasonable, and less intrusive, ways to protect the university, including blocking the suspect computer's Ethernet address. Finally, Savoy's searching wasn't limited to determining that the 117 computer was now 120. He did several searches, for 15 minutes, looking for incriminating files and making screen shots.

The larger problem may be that the court overlooked the fact that, regardless of what Savoy's stated motives were, it's clear that he searched a particular person's computer because he was suspicious of that person, and with the knowledge that whatever information he found he would give to law enforcement. Savoy may have been acting to protect the university, but he was also investigating the offense. That should have made his warrantless search unconstitutional.

While *U.S. v. Heckenkamp* says networked computers can be private, and applies the "special needs" exception in a narrow way, future prosecutors will try to expand it. Many searches in response to computer security breaches have dual purposes: fix the breach and make a case against the intruder. It will be hard for the courts to parse dual motivations to determine whether the *Heckenkamp* exception applies.

> "*[United States v. Heckenkamp states that] a student can consent to terms that render assertive security actions against him to be legal. So it would seem that similar terms could be consented to by the visitor to a Web site.*"

# The Principle of the Court's Decision Could Be Used to Fight Cybercrime

*Benjamin Wright*

*Benjamin Wright is an attorney and an instructor of courses on information security law for the SANS Technology Institute. In the following discussion he points out that a significant factor in the court's decision in* United States. v. Heckenkamp *was that by connecting his computer to the university network, Heckenkamp had assented to university policies. These policies allowed the university to execute security measures, even measures that compromised his usual rights under the law. In Wright's opinion, the same principle would apply if others, such as banks, took steps to investigate cybercrime after posting notices stating that by accessing their Web sites, users consented to security measures. This would allow site owners to employ investigative tactics that would otherwise violate the Wiretap Act and the Computer Fraud and Abuse Act.*

Benjamin Wright, "Can Cybercriminals Consent to Being Watched and Foiled?" SANS Technology Institute, May 14, 2007. Copyright © 2007 Benjamin Wright. Reproduced by permission of the author. http://benjaminwright.us.

Computer crime laws protect our use of the Internet, but they also raise issues for security professionals trying to thwart cyber criminals. For example, the federal Wiretap Act generally forbids the interception of electronic communications, and the federal Computer Fraud and Abuse Act generally prohibits entry into Internet computers without authority. These laws can cause a reputable professional to pause before probing a botnet [a collection of compromised computers running malicious software] too intrusively. These can also cause a bank security officer to hesitate before harassing a phishing site [a site that poses as another site in order to trick people into providing personal information] which is stealing bank customer user IDs and passwords. Were it not for the Computer Fraud and Abuse Act, the officer might be tempted to stuff the site with junk versions of those IDs and passwords.

From a security perspective, when something needs to be done about a botnet or a phishing site, the very laws that are supposed to fight cyber crime may on their face deter responsible defensive measures. Of course, instead of a professional taking steps on her own, she should consider calling law enforcement. But calling the police is not necessarily a satisfying option. The police do not always have the time, resources or jurisdiction to do something about every Internet criminal threat.

Yet if we conclude that nothing can be done about many criminal botnets and phishing, then we don't understand the full story.

## Consent to a Security Hack

Criminal law has long recognized that citizens are sometimes justified in taking limited measures against criminals. Concepts such as citizen's arrest, self-defense and abatement of a nuisance can serve as defenses to allegations that a citizen committed a crime when reacting to criminal activity. These concepts support reasonable actions by citizens, which are in proportion to the threat.

A related idea in criminal law is that of *consent*. If someone consents to you coming onto their property, then you are not committing the crime of trespass when you do enter the property. Consent was a relevant factor when a University of Wisconsin system administrator hacked into the personal computer of a student. According to a federal appeals court, the student consented to the hack.

The University of Wisconsin story happened like this: A university system administrator had good reason to believe that a certain personal computer, which was hooked to the university network, was a serious threat to a mail server on the network. So the administrator hacked into and gathered information about the PC. The information from the PC indicated that the student using it was engaged in illegal hacking activity around the Internet. This information led to the student's arrest and conviction. In *US v. Heckenkamp* the student argued that the administrator's hack into his machine violated his right to privacy (his 4th Amendment right to be free from unreasonable government searches). But the appellate court ruled that the administrator's actions did not violate the student's rights. A key reason cited by the court is that the student had consented to university policies when he attached his computer to the network and those policies recognized the right of the university to take limited security actions. The court said the administrator's hack was a reasonable security effort to protect the mail server that was under threat.

In other words, the court said the student made a bargain when he connected to the university's infrastructure. The bargain was that if the university allowed him to connect, then he allowed the university to execute security measures, even measures that compromised his usual rights under law. Thus the university could take steps against him that are normally illegal, but they were not illegal because the student had consented to them.

## Reasonable Limits to Consent

The concept of consent is important in the security field, but it is also tricky. It would be unfair, for instance, if a criminal could avoid being punished by forcing their victim to "consent" to a beating before she beat them. So the law places reasonable limits to the ability of people to consent to actions taken against them. These reasonable limits protect innocent people.

But, because the limits are based on reasonableness, they probably provide more protection to sympathetic people like consumers and less protection to people in less need of sympathy, such as corporations or aggressive cyber criminals.

## Practical Implications

Given what we've just learned about consent and criminal law, how can we apply it to efforts to stop botnets and phishers?

We've learned that a student can consent to terms that render assertive security actions against him to be legal. So it would seem that similar terms could be consented to by the visitor to a Web site. The terms might say, "by using our site you consent to us investigating and foiling any illegal activities by you connected with our site." By posting terms like these, a Web administrator is helping itself make a case that its security activities against visitors are within the law (although I've not yet found a judicial decision specifically confirming this interpretation of law).

Thus, it seems that a bank has incentive to post terms like these on its Web site: "If you access our site in connection with an effort to engage in phishing, then you consent to us surveilling, harassing and retaliating against your phishing activities." With terms like these, the bank is compiling evidence that it is within its rights to spy on phishers targeting it and to stuff their phishing sites with junk data. The bank is building the case that its justified security measures do not violate laws like the Wiretap Act and the Computer Fraud and Abuse Act.

# CHAPTER 3

# Cybercrimes Committed in One State Can Be Prosecuted by Another

# Case Overview

## *Hageseth v. San Mateo County* (2007)

Ordering prescription drugs over the Internet has become a common practice. It is entirely legal when a prescription from a patient's own physician is mailed or faxed to the pharmacy. But some online pharmacies offer to send medication to people who have not obtained prescriptions. Selling drugs without a prescription is illegal, but such pharmacies get around the law by contracting with doctors who agree to write prescriptions for patients they have never seen and about whom they know nothing.

In 2005 nineteen-year-old John McKay, a college student in California, purchased fluoxetine—a generic form of the antidepressant Prozac—from a Web site located in India. He filled out a questionnaire stating that he wanted the drug for "treatment for the symptoms of adult attention deficit disorder in relation to depression." It was sent to a company headquartered in Florida, which processed the order and sent it on to Colorado psychiatrist Dr. Christian Hageseth. After looking at John's questionnaire, Hageseth wrote a prescription and sent it to the Florida company's Texas server, which forwarded it to a pharmacy in Mississippi. The pharmacy filled the prescription and mailed it to McKay's California address.

There are many such transactions, and this one might never have attracted attention had it not been that seven weeks after he received the pills, John McKay committed suicide. He died from carbon monoxide poisoning after running a hose into his car from the exhaust, but traces of fluoxetine were found in his body. His father, who is a professor of molecular biology, believed that the drug contributed to his death.

McKay's parents filed suit against the online pharmacy, the pharmacy that filled the prescription, and Hageseth, but the court said they could not prove that the suicide had been caused by fluoxetine. Most experts do not believe that antidepressants cause direct harm, although the U.S. Food and Drug Administration now requires such drugs to carry a warning that they may lead to suicidal thoughts in children and young people.

However, doctors are not allowed to treat patients without examining them (except through legitimate telemedicine, which involves consultation with a local doctor). If they do, they can be fined and lose their licenses to practice. Furthermore, Hageseth, whose Colorado license was restricted because of unrelated misconduct, did not have a California medical license. So California authorities charged him with practicing medicine without a license, a felony for which he could be sent to prison.

Hageseth claimed that California had no jurisdiction over him because he had not been in California and thus had not practiced there. The case in this chapter is his appeal, in which the court ruled that crimes committed in cyberspace can be prosecuted by the state where they produce detrimental results. Because it was a California court, the ruling is not binding in other states. Online prescription of pharmaceuticals to strangers is a dangerous trend that many people feel can be dealt with only through federal legislation.

"The problem is unscrupulous, professionally negligent Internet physicians who blindly approve prescriptions for patients they know nothing about, with no regard for the risks or consequences, just to make some quick and easy money," John McKay's father wrote to the *Stanford Daily*. He hoped that Hageseth would be convicted so that a message would be sent to other doctors who are abusing the capabilities of the Internet. His hopes were fulfilled when Hageseth was sentenced to nine months in prison in April 2009.

"The Attorney General is himself not now willing to accept the view that unlawful Internet activity can only be addressed at the national or international level, and we have no basis upon which to say he is wrong."

# The Court's Opinion: Doctors Can Be Prosecuted for Prescribing over the Internet Without a License

## J. Anthony Kline

*J. Anthony Kline has been the presiding justice of the Court of Appeals of California, First District, Division Two since 1982. He is the cofounder of the San Francisco Conservation Corps, which was the first urban municipal youth corps in the nation. In the following opinion in* Hageseth v. San Mateo County, *he rules that Dr. Christian Hageseth can be tried for practicing medicine without a license in California even though he was not in California at the time he prescribed medication over the Internet for a California teenager he had never seen. Furthermore, Justice Kline says, it makes no difference that the crime was committed in cyberspace. Although Hageseth claimed he had not been told it was illegal to prescribe for a patient outside the state in which he was licensed, that was something he should have known, according to Kline. His claim that for him to be prosecuted by an individual state would not deter others from breaking the law is*

J. Anthony Kline, opinion, *Christian Ellis Hageseth v. Superior Court of San Mateo County*, Court of Appeals of California, First District, Division Two, May 21, 2007. Reproduced by permission.

*not valid because technology for finding doctors who prescribe il-
legally over the Internet is being developed and not punishing
them would give them greater freedom to do it than they already
possess. And there is no danger that prosecuting such cases will
stifle the development of telemedicine, Kline affirms, since the
California law specifically allows out-of-state doctors to practice
if they are in consultation with a California doctor.*

This writ petition presents the question whether a defendant who was never himself physically present in this
state at any time during the commission of the criminal offense with which he is charged, and did not act through an
agent ever present in this state, is subject to the criminal jurisdiction of respondent court even though no jurisdictional
statute specifically extends the extraterritorial jurisdiction of
California courts for the particular crime with which he is
charged. . . .

Petitioner, whose allegedly unlawful conduct consisted entirely of Internet-mediated communications, claims the trial
court lacks jurisdiction because no part of that conduct took
place within the State of California. . . .

On or about June 11, 2005, John McKay, a resident of San
Mateo County, initiated an online purchase of fluoxetine
(generic Prozac) on www.usanetrx.com, an interactive Web
site located outside of the United States. The questionnaire
McKay received and returned online, which identified him as
a resident of this state, was forwarded by operators of the Web
site to JRB Health Solutions (JRB) for processing. JRB, which
has its headquarters in Florida and operates a server in Texas,
forwarded McKay's purchase request and questionnaire to petitioner, its "physician subcontractor," who resided in Fort
Collins, Colorado, and was then licensed to practice medicine
in that state. After reviewing McKay's answers to the questionnaire, petitioner issued an online prescription of the requested
medication and returned it to JRB's server in Texas. JRB then
forwarded the prescription to the Gruich Pharmacy Shoppe in

Biloxi, Mississippi, which filled the prescription and mailed the requested amount of fluoxetine to McKay at his California address. Several weeks later, intoxicated on alcohol and with a detectable amount of fluoxetine in his blood, McKay committed suicide by means of carbon monoxide poisoning. The Board's report indicates, and it is undisputed, that petitioner was at all material times located in Colorado and never directly communicated with anyone in California regarding the prescription. His communications were only with JRB, from whom he received McKay's online request for fluoxetine and questionnaire, and to whom he sent the prescription he issued.

On May 24, 2006, the district attorney filed a criminal complaint charging that, "in the County of San Mateo," petitioner willfully and unlawfully practiced medicine in this state without a valid license authorizing him to do so, in violation of Business and Professions Code section 2052, a felony. On the same date, the trial court issued a warrant for petitioner's arrest and admitting him to bail in the amount of $500,000. . . .

## California Has Jurisdiction

Penal Code section 27 generally permits the punishment of a defendant under California law for any crime committed 'in whole or in part' in the state. . . .

With the parties, we agree that the jurisdictional statutes applicable to this case are section 27, subdivision (a)(1), and section 778. . . .

Petitioner maintains he committed no "part" of the offense in California, as section 27 requires, and does not come within the purview of section 778 because he did not use an "agent or some other means" to consummate a crime in California. Petitioner maintains that his "act of practicing medicine began and ended with the writing of the prescription in Colorado," and "[t]he filling of the prescription, which occurred in Mississippi, was an entirely separate act, requiring a separate license," for which he cannot be held criminally accountable. As petitioner sees the matter, it is irrelevant whether he knew the medication he prescribed would be sent to California because his act ended with the writing of the prescription, and section 778 does not make his knowledge of the fact that the medication he prescribed would be sent to California a determining or even a relevant factor. . . .

[In *People v. Jones* (2003)] we viewed section 778 as showing "legislative recognition of the concept that a defendant may violate a California penal statute even though outside of the state at the time of its commission", and as consistent with the rule of *Strassheim v. Daily* (1911) that a state may exercise jurisdiction over criminal acts that are committed outside the state but are intended to, and do, produce harm within the state. . . .

*People v. Lazarevich* (2004) employed a similar analysis. The defendant in that case was tried and convicted of maliciously depriving the mother of her custodial rights regarding the couple's child in violation of section 278.5 and a court order by taking them out of the country and secreting them in Serbia. . . . The *Lazarevich* court concluded that "California has jurisdiction of defendant's act of withholding his children in Serbia because his failure to abide by a valid California child custody order constitutes an act or omission outside of the country that necessarily produced *a substantial detrimental effect in California,* and defendant obviously knew that his withholding his children from his former wife produced territorial effects in California."

## Physical Presence Unnecessary

The "the objective territorial principle" or "detrimental effects" theory of extraterritorial criminal jurisdiction, which evolved out of the common law view of territorial jurisdiction, was most authoritatively articulated by Justice [Oliver Wendell] Holmes in *Strassheim v. Daily.* The defendant in that case, Daily, who resided in Illinois, offered to bribe Armstrong, the warden of a state prison in Michigan, if he agreed to accept machinery required by contract to be new but which Armstrong knew was used. Daily offered the bribe while he was in Illinois, though he made several visits to Michigan in pursuit of the contract. Assuming that, other than those visits, Daily did no act in Michigan connected with his plan, Justice Holmes concluded that "[i]f a jury should believe the evidence and find that Daily did the acts that led Armstrong to betray his trust, deceived the Board of Control, and induced by fraud the payment by the State, the usage of the civilized world would warrant Michigan in punishing him, *although he never had set foot in the State until after the fraud was complete. Acts done outside a jurisdiction, but intended to produce and producing detrimental effects within it, justify a State in punishing the cause of the harm as if he had been present at the effect, if the State should succeed in getting him within its power."*

Though Justice Holmes's opinion acknowledged the several visits Daily made to Michigan, the italicized language, which requires no act in the forum state [the state where the court is located] has been treated by modern courts as a reasonable and sufficient basis upon which to confer territorial jurisdiction. . . .

The detrimental effect theory of extraterritorial jurisdiction has been described as a "doctrine of constructive presence," a legal fiction considered "necessary to the practical administration of criminal justice." (*State v. Winkler*). Under this common law rule, "if a man in the state of South Carolina criminally fires a ball into the state of Georgia, the law regards him as accompanying the ball, and as being represented by it, up to the point where it strikes." (*Simpson v. State*).

The detrimental effect theory of extraterritorial jurisdiction has been incorporated into the Model Penal Code and has been accepted by our Supreme Court as a valid basis upon which territorial jurisdiction may be posited. Section

778 essentially codifies this theory of extraterritorial criminal jurisdiction. The statute renders a person liable to punishment for the commission of a public offense "commenced without the State" if the offense is "consummated within its boundaries" through the intervention of an agent or "other means proceeding directly from said defendant." As discussed above, the text of the statute does not require that the agent or "other means" by which the crime is committed be within the forum state. . . .

In short, it is not necessary to the "detrimental effect" theory of extraterritorial jurisdiction that the defendant be physically present in this state during some portion of the time during which his alleged criminal act took place, or that he act through an agent physically present in this state, or that there exist a statute or judicially declared exception extending the state's territorial jurisdiction for the particular crime with which the defendant is charged. Accordingly, in the circumstances of this case, jurisdiction is not precluded by petitioner's physical absence from the state and the fact he did not act through an agent located in California. . . .

## Practicing Without a License

The charged offense, violation of section 2052 of the Business and Professions Code, prohibits the act of holding oneself out "as practicing any system or mode of treating the sick or afflicted in this state," or practicing such a system or mode of treatment by "diagnos[ing], treat[ing], operat[ing] for, or prescrib[ing] for any . . . physical or mental condition of any person," without having at the time of doing so a valid license. The criminalization of these acts represents a reasonable exercise of the state police power, as the statute was designed to prevent the provision of medical treatment to residents of the state by persons who are inadequately trained or otherwise incompetent to provide such treatment, and who have not subjected themselves to the regulatory regime established by the

Medical Practice Act. Causing or intending an injury is not an element of the offense; and the injury sought to be prevented could not occur in another jurisdiction. A preponderance of the evidence shows that, without having at the time a valid California medical license, petitioner prescribed fluoxetine for a person he knew to be a California resident knowing that act would cause the prescribed medication to be sent to that person at the California address he provided. If the necessary facts can be proved at trial beyond a reasonable doubt, the People will have satisfactorily shown a violation of Business and Professions Code section 2052. It is enough for our purposes that a preponderance of the evidence now shows that petitioner intended to produce or could reasonably foresee that his act would produce, and he did produce, the detrimental effect section 2052 was designed to prevent.

Petitioner endeavors to diminish the significance of the nature and intentionality of his act by focusing almost entirely on the requirement of section 778 that the act be "consummated" within the boundaries of this state. According to petitioner, no criminal act can be "consummated" in California unless the actor or his agent is present here at some point between the commencement of the criminal act and its completion, and that is not here the case. Petitioner may be right with respect to some criminal acts, but his theory does not apply to all, because not all crimes are necessarily "consummated" upon completion by the actor of the last element of the offense. . . . In its common meaning, consummation denotes completion. In many instances, of course, a crime is completed upon commission of the last element of the required *actus reus* ["guilty act"]. Where, however, a statute, in addition to prohibiting conduct, includes within its definition of the offense a specific result, then the crime is not completed until that result occurs. And if the prohibited result occurs in a place other than the conduct which occasioned it, the location of the result may fairly be deemed the place where the crime is 'consummated.' . . .

A preponderance of the evidence shows petitioner prescribed medication for a resident of this state, aware of the virtual certainty his conduct would cause the prescribed medication to be sent that person at his residence in California. This state is thus the place where the crime is "consummated." The fact that other parts of the crime were committed elsewhere is immaterial, as there is no constitutional or other reason "that prevents a state from punishing, as an offense against the penal laws of such state, a crime when only a portion of the acts constituting the crime are committed within the state." (*People v. Botkin*). Accordingly, respondent court possesses the necessary jurisdiction.

Jurisdiction is not defeated by the fact that petitioner consummated the charged offense through the use of intermediaries located in other states. The trial court indicated its belief that a person in Colorado commits a crime in California if he sends a bomb through the mail that explodes when the addressee opens the package in California. Petitioner's counsel agreed that might be true, but distinguished the situation here because it was not petitioner, but the Mississippi pharmacy, that sent the prescription to California, and petitioner "had no contact at all with Mr. McKay." The mere fact that petitioner acted through intermediaries—whether they be deemed "agent[s] or any other means"—is irrelevant under section 778: All that is required by the statute is that the intervention of such intermediaries "proceed[] directly from" petitioner, as a preponderance of the evidence shows it did. . . .

For the foregoing reasons, and because a preponderance of the evidence now shows that petitioner's acts outside this state were intended to produce and produced detrimental effects within it, we believe the objective territorial principle codified by section 778 provides a basis upon which jurisdiction might be found to lie in this case. Indeed, if petitioner's communications had been by letter or telephone facsimile, there is little doubt where jurisdiction would lie.

The remaining question is whether it should make a difference that petitioner's offense took place in cyberspace rather than in the real space for which the jurisdictional statutes were designed.

## Cybercrime Can Be Traditional Crime

"Cybercrime" relates not just to the unauthorized use or disruption of computer files or programs and the theft of an electronic identity, but also to the use of a computer to facilitate or carry out a traditional criminal offense, as alleged in this case. This species of cybercrime is considered by some no different from crimes committed in real space, and this school feels it should therefore be regulated in the same manner. However, a growing number believe cyberspace requires a different system of rules, particularly with respect to jurisdictional issues. Jurisdictional doctrine, which is constitutionally grounded in the due process clause of the Fourteenth Amendment, is not static. Jurisdictional principles have been adjusted to accommodate evolving social, economic, and political needs, and the Supreme Court has long also "recognized that personal jurisdiction must adapt to progress in technology." (*Weber v. Jolly Hotels*). Mindful of the dynamic relationship between law and technology, some maintain that "[t]he modern development of the Internet represents just the type of technological change that calls for the doctrinal modification traditionally characterizing both the common law process of constitutional interpretation in general and the law of personal jurisdiction in particular." (Redish, *Of New Wine and Old Bottles*).

An aspect of Internet technology that assertedly most warrants modification of jurisdictional doctrine is the extent to which it undermines the role of territorial boundaries in delineating "law space"—that is, in providing notice that the crossing of a physical boundary may subject one to new rules. It is said that "[c]yberspace radically undermines the relationship between legally significant (online) phenomena and physical location. The rise of the global computer network is destroying the link between geographical location and: (1) the power of local governments to assert control over online behavior; (2) the effects of online behavior on individuals or things; (3) the legitimacy of a local sovereign's efforts to regulate global phenomena; and (4) the ability of physical location to give notice of which sets of rules apply. The Net thus radically subverts the system of rule-making based on borders between physical spaces, at least with respect to the claim that Cyberspace should naturally be governed by territorially defined rules." (Johnson & Post, *Law and Borders: The Rise of Law in Cyberspace*). For these reasons, it is claimed that governmental efforts "to map local regulation and physical boundaries into Cyberspace" are sure to prove quixotic [unreachably idealistic]; and the Internet must be therefore left alone to "develop its own effective legal institutions".

While Internet technology can create new realities courts may be compelled to accommodate, those who claim their Internet-related conduct should be exempt from a traditional legal principle because the conduct is not within the paradigm for which the rule was designed bear the burden of establishing the fact. Petitioner has not done so.

Petitioner does not make the bold claim that cyberspace is or should be beyond the reach of the criminal law, but he does insist that the People's assertion of extraterritorial jurisdiction over his Internet conduct is unreasonable because (1) he and others are not on notice of the unlawfulness of such conduct, and (2) the assertion of jurisdiction would not deter others from his allegedly unlawful conduct, but (3) it would deter physicians licensed in other states from providing residents of this state many useful forms of medical assistance over the Internet.

The claim that petitioner and others like him who prescribe medications over the Internet lack notice of the unlawfulness of that conduct is unacceptable. California's proscription of the unlicensed practice of medicine is neither an obscure nor an unusual state prohibition of which ignorance can reasonably be claimed, and certainly not by persons like petitioner who are licensed health care providers. Nor can such persons reasonably claim ignorance of the fact that authorization of a prescription pharmaceutical constitutes the practice of medicine.

The claim that a finding of jurisdiction in this case would not deter out-of-state physicians from prescribing medications for residents of this state via the Internet cannot be so easily dismissed. Such physicians or the Web sites that employ them can and usually do conceal their names, locations, and state of licensure and it is difficult and costly for regulatory and law enforcement agencies to discover this information, as they must in order to charge a person with the unlawful practice of medicine.

## Deterring Illegal Online Prescribing

Nonetheless, as this case demonstrates, the information can sometimes be discovered; so that federal and state agencies are not invariably unable to find and assert jurisdiction to punish persons and entities engaged in the unlawful prescription of pharmaceuticals over the Internet. In an amicus [friend of the court] brief in behalf of himself and the Medical Board of California, the Attorney General represents that the Board is actively engaged in investigating the significant number of complaints it receives about the unlawful prescription of drugs by means of the Internet for residents of this state by physicians not licensed here, and has had "some success" in constraining this practice. The Attorney General is himself not now willing to accept the view that unlawful Internet activity can only be addressed at the national or international level, and we have no basis upon which to say he is wrong.

Given the absence at this time of any significant national or international effort to deter the widespread and growing use of the Internet to sell drugs without a prescription made on the basis of a good faith hands-on medical examination by a physician licensed in the state in which the patient resides (or without any prescription at all), the denial of state jurisdiction to punish the practice would provide the unscrupulous physicians who engage in it even greater freedom to do so than they already possess. Moreover, while state efforts to identify and obtain personal jurisdiction over such physicians are now often frustrated by Internet technology, technological innovations, network engineering, and Internet intermediaries are making it easier to identify and locate those whose unlawful acts take place in cyberspace and to enforce the law. Web sites and Internet service providers already possess the ability to design or filter content based on user location, and at least one state court has issued an enforceable order directing a provider of prescription pharmaceuticals to cease delivering unlawfully prescribed drugs into the forum state, and to place notice on its Web site that it will not do so. The prospect of other technological developments counsels judicial caution in accepting technology-based arguments against the assertion of jurisdiction, as that would eliminate incentives for technology developers to innovate in ways that would facilitate law enforcement and support public values.

Finally, there appears to be little danger that the finding of extraterritorial jurisdiction in this case will stifle provision over the Internet of many useful forms of medical assistance to residents of this state in need thereof. The practice of "telemedicine"—i.e., "health care delivery, diagnosis, consultation, treatment, transfer of medical data, and education using interactive audio, video, or data communications"—is specifically authorized by the Telemedicine Development Act of 1996. Furthermore, the Medical Practice Act exempts from the unlawful practice of medicine "a practitioner located outside this state, when in actual consultation, whether within this state or across state lines, with a licensed practitioner of this state" provided only that the out-of-state practitioner does not "appoint a place to meet patients [in this state], receive calls from patients within the limits of this state, give orders, or have ultimate authority over the care or primary diagnosis of a patient who is located within this state."

In short, there is no persuasive reason why petitioner's or his employer's use of cyberspace, or the use of it by McKay or the Web site he contacted, should defeat application in this case of the traditional legal principles we rely upon to find extraterritorial jurisdiction.

> *"Criminal prosecution—or even the threat of prosecution—is 'a critical element of the [medical] board's efforts to deter . . . Internet prescribing.'"*

# Prosecution Will Deter Online Prescribing of Drugs to Patients Doctors Have Not Examined

## Bob Egelko

*Bob Egelko is a staff writer for* The San Francisco Chronicle. *In the following article he reports on the case* Hageseth v. San Mateo County, *which involved prescription of drugs over the Internet by an out-of-state doctor. Colorado physician Christian Hageseth prescribed an antidepressant for a California teenager he had never seen via an order from an online pharmacy. After the boy killed himself, his father complained to the state medical board, which led authorities to prosecute Hageseth even though he did not write the prescription in California. When he claimed that they had no jurisdiction over him, the court of appeals ruled that he could be prosecuted in California because he had known the medication would be delivered there. He was not charged with causing the boy's death, but only with practicing medicine in California without a license; however, that is a felony. He pleaded no contest and was sentenced to nine months in jail in April 2009. The victim's father believes his conviction should send a message to the many other doctors who are prescribing online for patients they know almost nothing about.*

Bob Egelko, "Father Blames Son's Suicide on 'Telemedicine,'" *San Francisco Chronicle,* December 29, 2008. Copyright © 2008 Hearst Communications Inc., Hearst Newspaper Division. Reproduced by permission.

In August 2005, John McKay, a 19-year-old Stanford student and former high school debate champion, committed suicide by rolling up the windows in a car at his mother's Menlo Park home and piping in exhaust fumes.

In the next few weeks, a Colorado doctor who had prescribed a generic form of Prozac for McKay after receiving his request over the Internet, without ever seeing or examining him, will go on trial in Redwood City on possibly precedent-setting charges of practicing medicine in California without a license.

A conviction of Dr. Christian Hageseth, 67, "would send a clear message to those individuals who are blindly writing prescriptions to patients they know nothing about," said the youth's father, David McKay, a former Stanford professor now living in Colorado. They would have to ask themselves, he said, "whether quick and easy money is worth the risk of a criminal conviction and permanent loss of their medical license."

Hageseth's lawyer, Carleton Briggs, sees the issue differently. The case may determine, he said, whether California can reach across state lines to prosecute practitioners of "telemedicine," an increasingly common source of health care. "A lot of medication is prescribed over the Internet," Briggs said. "Can California regulate it in this fashion?... No out-of-state telemedicine provider has ever been jailed for practicing medicine in California."

So far, though, courts have rejected Briggs' attempts to get the charge dismissed, including a civil suit claiming the prosecution is an unconstitutional attempt by California to regulate interstate commerce. A San Mateo County Superior Court judge threw the suit out Dec. 17, but Briggs said he'll raise the issue in an appeal if Hageseth is convicted.

## No Federal Regulation

The case has already had a legal impact. In a May 2007 ruling against Hageseth, the First District Court of Appeal in San

Francisco said a California county can prosecute someone who writes a prescription in another state for a Californian, knowing that the medicine will be delivered in this state.

In the absence of any federal regulation of unlicensed drug prescription and sales over the Internet, "the denial of state jurisdiction to punish the practice would provide the unscrupulous physicians who engage in it even greater freedom to do so," said Presiding Justice J. Anthony Kline. He noted that state law allows out-of-state doctors to practice "telemedicine" through the Internet or interactive audio or video transmissions, as long as they act in consultation with a licensed California physician.

San Mateo County authorities were alerted to the case by the state Medical Board, which receives nearly 20 complaints a year about Internet prescriptions, the board's executive director, David Thornton, said in an April 2007 court declaration in Hageseth's case. At first, he said, the prescriptions were mostly for "lifestyle drugs" such as Viagra and medication to stop hair loss, but lately they've included more addictive and dangerous substances.

Licensed California doctors can be disciplined in such cases for failure to conduct an appropriate examination before prescribing, Thornton said. And any prescriber, licensed or not, can be fined as much as $25,000 per incident.

Enforcement of civil penalties in other states is often problematic, however, and criminal prosecution—or even the threat of prosecution—is "a critical element of the board's efforts to deter such Internet prescribing," Thornton said.

## McKay Ordered Drug Online

John McKay had just completed his freshman year at Stanford in June 2005 when he ordered 90 capsules of the antidepressant fluoxetine, the generic version of Prozac, from the India-based Web site *usanetrx.com*. In a questionnaire that accompanied the order, he said he would use the drug to treat "adult attention deficit disorder in relation to depression" and also said he was not suicidal.

The site operator forwarded the order to a Texas company, JRB Solutions, which relayed it to Hageseth, its physician contractor in Fort Collins, Colorado. Hageseth quickly filled the prescription without contacting McKay and returned it to JRB, which had the pills shipped to Menlo Park from a pharmacy in Mississippi.

At the time, the U.S. Food and Drug Administration [FDA] required Prozac and similar antidepressants to carry warning labels saying they increased the risk of suicidal thoughts and behavior in children and adolescents. The FDA asked manufacturers in 2007 to expand the warning to cover patients ages 18 to 24 in the early weeks of treatment, but that won't affect the criminal case against Hageseth, who is charged only with practicing medicine illegally and not with prescribing the wrong drug or causing McKay's death.

Traces of fluoxetine were found in McKay's body after his death, along with alcohol. In a civil suit by his parents against the Mississippi pharmacy, JRB and Hageseth, however, a federal judge said experts on both sides of the case had concluded the drug was not a cause of his death.

McKay's father remains unconvinced. "I have strong opinions about how the drug was affecting my son. You can't do a post mortem diagnosis, but I think it was driving him off the deep end," said David McKay, who was a Stanford professor of molecular biology at the time of his son's death and is now a research professor at the University of Colorado.

"The real problem is negligence on the part of the physician," he said. "Any competent psychiatrist talking to [John McKay] for five minutes on the telephone would have realized something was wrong and would have encouraged him to seek direct help."

McKay's parents settled their suits against the pharmacy and JRB and dropped their suit against Hageseth, who surrendered his Colorado medical license after coming under investigation in the youth's suicide.

## The Prosecutors' Challenge

In contrast to the civil suit, which would have required the parents to prove that Hageseth's actions contributed to their son's death, San Mateo County prosecutors must show only that he practiced medicine in California without a license. A conviction can be punished as either a misdemeanor, with as much as a year in jail, or as a felony, with as much as three years in prison.

The trial is scheduled Feb. 9, but defense attorney Briggs said he will ask for a 30-day delay because Hageseth recently underwent open-heart surgery.

He said it's far from an open-and-shut case—it's not clear, he said, that John McKay was even in California when he sent the order, or that the law makes it a crime for an out-of-state doctor to fill a California prescription.

What's more, Briggs said, any conviction under state law will be constitutionally dubious. "The Internet is an instrument of interstate commerce," he said. "The federal government has to regulate it if it is to be regulated."

Deputy Attorney General Catherine Rivlin said the appeals court laid that argument to rest by observing that doctors who prescribe for patients in California, without the required license, subject themselves to prosecution in the state. "How they were connected, whether it's a phone line or a computer, totally doesn't matter," Rivlin said.

Besides, she said, "There are certain parts of medicine, like prescribing dangerous drugs, that can't be done over the Internet. Medicine's still primarily a hands-on business, or it should be."

▎ *"The Internet flattens the world."*

# Legal Experts Disagree on Whether the Internet Demands New Rules About Territorial Boundaries

*Matthew Hirsch*

*The following article is a report on* Hageseth v. Superior Court (The People), *a case in which a doctor in Colorado prescribed drugs over the Internet to a teenager in California whom he had never seen. Because soon afterward the boy committed suicide, California prosecutors charged Dr. Christian Hageseth with the felony of practicing medicine without a state license. The doctor argued that because he had not been in California when he wrote the prescription, it had no jurisdiction over him. But the California Court of Appeals ruled against him, saying that according to the law a defendant can be prosecuted in California for a crime that starts outside the state if it is consummated within the state. It held that there is no reason why the use of cyberspace should make any difference.*

Two years ago, Christian Hageseth logged on to the Internet in Colorado and prescribed antidepressant drugs to a Menlo Park teenager with a history of mental illness and alcohol abuse. A few months later, 19-year-old John McKay killed himself in his family home.

Upon learning that Hageseth had treated McKay, and that he didn't have a license here, state medical investigators urged local prosecutors to charge him with a felony. Last year they did, accusing him of practicing without a California license. The maximum penalty, according to the prosecution, would be three years in state prison and state fines.

And although Hageseth's lawyer and deputy district attorneys in San Mateo County disagree on many aspects of the case, this much is clear: The 66-year-old Hageseth would be an easier target for prosecutors had he run his virtual doctor's office inside California state lines.

Now Hageseth—who had a restricted license in Colorado when he prescribed McKay's medication, according to court documents—is trying to get the case dismissed, claiming that the state courts lack jurisdiction to try him under California law. Though a San Mateo County judge refused his request, Hageseth's attorney, Santa Rosa lawyer Carleton Briggs, has persuaded the First District Court of Appeal to consider issuing a writ that would overturn that decision.

Briggs claims that if the First District agrees with the government's application of medical licensing laws, thousands of out-of-state doctors could face felony prosecution.

"The decision in this case will shape the future of telemedicine [in California]," Briggs wrote in his petition to the appeal court.

On that point, at least, Briggs seems to have found some agreement on the appeal court. At oral arguments in March, one justice suggested the case could have big repercussions, according to a transcript of the recorded argument, provided by Briggs.

"There are probably thousands, maybe hundreds of thousands of doctors in the 49 other states who are not licensed in this state, but who are providing some kind of medical attention for California residents," said the justice, who Briggs later identified as Justice J. Anthony Kline.

The appeal court took the rare step of asking for additional briefing on the court's jurisdiction over out-of-state doctors, suggesting the parties might want to seek out *amici* like the Medical Board of California.

Justices Kline, Paul Haerle and James Richman are expected to take *Hageseth v. Superior Court (The People)*, A115390, under submission at the end of the week.

## Medicine From Afar

Telemedicine refers to the delivery of medicine from afar, and it can occur in many ways. The broad term might refer to two doctors discussing a case over the phone or the Internet, for example. Or it might involve direct patient interaction with physicians located far away.

The American Telemedicine Association doesn't keep hard statistics on how many doctors incorporate telemedicine into their practice, according to the executive director, Jonathan Linkous.

But Susan Penney, a lawyer at the California Medical Association, said she thinks it's uncommon for doctors to prescribe medication without first meeting a patient face to face.

State law requires medical practitioners to conduct a good-faith exam before prescribing medication, Penney said. The CMA declined to weigh in with an *amicus* brief on Hageseth's behalf, she said, because Hageseth's position appears to be inconsistent with that requirement.

"We do not believe that we can support [Hageseth's] underlying position ... that it's appropriate to prescribe without a good-faith prior exam," she said.

In court papers, Hageseth claims the teenager wrote in his questionnaire that he had been prescribed antidepressants before, and that he neglected to mention his alcohol use. But prosecutors counter that this argument is a gratuitous attack on the victim, not to mention irrelevant because the doctor did nothing to verify McKay's claims.

Briggs said his client surrendered his Colorado license after medical officials there contacted him about McKay.

"Hageseth doesn't take the position that what he did is right. He takes the position that he did not commit a crime," Briggs said.

## Routing The Order

Hageseth hooked up with McKay in June 2005 through an overseas Web site called Usanetrx.com, an Internet portal offering access to discount prescription drugs.

After transmitting his credit card number and some details about his medical history, McKay placed an order for fluoxetine, a generic alternative to Prozac.

The order was then routed through JRB Health Solutions, a Florida company with which Hageseth worked to prescribe medication. A Mississippi pharmacy used by JRB then filled McKay's order and shipped the meds directly to him.

A few weeks later, after McKay committed suicide by carbon monoxide poisoning, alcohol and fluoxetine were detected in his bloodstream.

Last year, McKay's parents sued Hageseth, JRB Health Solutions and the Mississippi pharmacy, among others, in California's Northern District federal court. That case is still pending. But so far Hageseth is the only defendant who's faced criminal prosecution, according to his lawyer.

Briggs argues that the state's licensing requirements don't apply to Hageseth because he never set foot in California while acting as McKay's doctor.

"If anything, it was McKay who left California via the Internet and went to India," where Usanetrx.com is registered, Briggs said.

San Mateo County Deputy District Attorney Jennifer Ow, who wrote one of the briefs opposing Briggs' writ petition, said it might be true that McKay left the state via the Internet—but Hageseth then would have entered the state the same way.

"The Internet flattens the world," she said.

In court papers, Briggs argues that if the prosecution's position becomes law, "any out-of-state doctor practicing telemedicine for a California resident can be arrested anywhere in the country, handcuffed and extradited . . . to face felony charges."

Ow has countered in her briefs that Briggs' "rhetoric sounds compelling," but she maintains that Hageseth's use of the Internet cannot shield him from liability.

She draws a comparison to a hypothetical person from Colorado who plans to have his estranged wife killed in California, then argues that California courts have jurisdiction only over the hit man. "Such a result is ludicrous," she wrote.

The deputy DA also argues that Hageseth's challenge "strikes at the very heart" of Penal Code § 778, a law tailored specifically to allow the prosecution of a defendant from another state who commits a crime in California.

The state attorney general's office, responding to the appeal court's invitation to submit a brief on the jurisdiction question, has supported the DA's position.

Deputy Attorney General Catherine Rivlin wrote that Briggs' vision of out-of-state physicians being dragged off to jail is "unfounded."

She noted, for example, that state law exempts out-of-state doctors from the licensing requirement if they are acting in consultation with a licensed California physician. What's more, she added, the state's licensing requirement "has not filled jails with well-meaning unlicensed practitioners."

Briggs said he accepts that out-of-state doctors treating people in California without a license in this state have largely escaped scrutiny so far. Those physicians haven't been filling the jails "because they haven't prosecuted anybody," he added. "This is the first time."

*"When professionals offer services online [to] consumers in other jurisdictions, it will be simpler to refer to a uniform federal law than to fight over which state's law applies."*

# Federal Regulation of Online Prescribing May Replace State Laws

*Anita Ramasastry*

*Anita Ramasastry is an associate professor of law at the University of Washington School of Law. In the following viewpoint she discusses* Hageseth v. San Mateo County, *a case in which a Colorado doctor prescribed medication over the Internet to a California teenager whom he had never seen and who later died. The California Court of Appeals ruled that the doctor could be prosecuted for practicing medicine without a California license, and some people have feared that this decision may discourage the use of the Internet for legitimate medical purposes. However, Ramasastry points out that California law specifically allows for the practice of telemedicine by out-of-state doctors who are in consultation with a California doctor. Also, patients can still have prescriptions filled by out-of-state online pharmacies if they fax or mail a prescription from a local doctor. Eventually she says, there will probably be a federal law to regulate online prescription practices that will supersede state laws. One law that*

*Congress is considering, she notes, would require the pharmacy to have a prescription from a doctor who has conducted an in-person evaluation of the patient.*

Congress is currently considering new legislation that would crack down on online pharmacies that provide prescription medications without patients having to visit a physician.

Meanwhile, a California court recently [in 2007] cracked down in its own way—holding that a Colorado physician, lacking a California license, could be prosecuted for prescribing medication online to a California resident whom he had never met, and who subsequently died.

In this column, I'll discuss the California holding—which, while in my view [is] correct; probably will not have far-reaching consequences. In addition, I'll describe some of the proposals Congress is deciding [on] whether to enact into law.

## The Facts of the California Case

In June 2005, after finishing his freshman year at Stanford, John McKay accessed an overseas online pharmacy portal, US-Anetrx.com, which reportedly told customers they could obtain prescription drugs "without the embarrassment of talking to a doctor." Unlike most online pharmacies, this site did not require a faxed or mailed prescription from a licensed pharmacist.

McKay ordered 90 capsules of the antidepressant Prozac (generic name "fluoxetine") after transmitting his credit card and some medical history through an online questionnaire. The order was routed through JRB Health Solutions, a Florida company. One of JRB's subcontractors, Colorado physician Dr. Christian Hageseth, then authorized the prescription, without speaking to McKay. A Mississippi-based pharmacy used by JRB then filled the prescription and sent the medication to McKay in California. Subsequently, on August 2, 2005, with fluoxetine in his system, McKay—in an apparent suicide—died of carbon monoxide and alcohol poisoning.

## Civil Lawsuit and Criminal Prosecution

Under California Business and Professions Code 2242.1, the state prohibits the prescription and administration of a drug without a "good faith" prior examination and medical indication.

[In 2006], McKay's parents brought a wrongful death suit against Hageseth, JRB Health, and the Mississippi pharmacy, among others, in the U.S. District Court for the Northern District of California. . . .

In addition, Hageseth is now facing criminal prosecution in California for practicing without a California license—a felony that carries a jail sentence. Dr. Hageseth's asserted defense is that California's licensing requirements don't apply because he never set foot in California while acting as McKay's doctor. For this reason, he says, he never practiced medicine in California.

Hageseth recently tried to get the criminal case dismissed, claiming that California courts lacked jurisdiction. After losing his motion before a San Mateo County judge, he went to the First District Court of Appeal.

## Jurisdiction Exists for the Prosecution

The California Court of Appeals, however, found that Hageseth was indeed subject to prosecution in California, under traditional legal principles governing extraterritorial jurisdiction.

Section 778 of the California Penal Code recognizes jurisdiction for criminal offenses when a crime is committed in whole or in part in California. The court held that the crime against McKay was indeed committed in part in California, employing the concept of "constructive presence."

This concept holds that a person may be subject to punishment not only for an offense he himself commits in California, but also for an offense consummated within California's boundaries by his agent or by "other means" proceeding directly from him. In this case, the court pointed out that the Mississippi pharmacy acted as Hageseth's agent in filling his prescription, and that the pharmacies or its agencies sent the drugs to McKay in California. It was immaterial that the agent was located outside of California since its actions had a detrimental impact inside California.

The court specifically noted that "it makes no difference that the charged conduct took place in cyberspace, rather than real space." The key was that the conduct had detrimental effects in California, and was directed at California.

## Not as Far-Reaching as Some Suggest

Some observers have complained that the California ruling may deter other doctors from offering valuable medical services using the Internet. However, the California court pointed out that telemedicine legislation in California specifically allows for certain kinds of medical consultation to occur via interactive telephonic, video and Internet media. In addition, the State's Medical Practice Act specifically exempts practitioners from licensing requirements when they act across state lines, if they are doing so in consultation with another physician who is licensed in California.

Observers have also expressed fears that this decision will lessen consumers' online access to lower-cost prescription drugs. But consumers can still use the procedure many online pharmacies already require—of obtaining a prescription from a local doctor and faxing or mailing it in.

Finally, observers have worried that this decision will open the door for overreaching in other contexts. What if California (or another state) decides to label other out-of-state conduct a crime; show that it has a detrimental effect in California; and then indict the out-of-stater? As [computer crime law expert] Orin Kerr has noted, however, the dormant commerce clause doctrine may serve as a valid check on overreaching. (The Commerce Clause empowers Congress to regulate interstate commerce; the dormant commerce clause limits individual states' interference with interstate commerce.)

## National Laws Will Supersede State Laws

In the end, federal (and international) solutions will probably be superior. When professionals offer services online [to] consumers in other jurisdictions, it will be simpler to refer to a uniform federal law than to fight over which state's law applies. No wonder, then, that in the Hageseth case, the court noted that it was acting "[g]iven the absence at this time of any significant national or international effort to counter the widespread and growing use of the Internet to sell drugs without a prescription based on a good faith hands-on medical examination by a physician licensed in the state in which the patient resides (or without any prescription at all . . .)."

What should the federal law mandate? In some cases, requiring personal or at verbal or visual contact may be desirable. Surely, for example, getting a prescription should require more than an intake form if at all possible.

One law Congress is considering—the proposed Online Pharmacy Consumer Protection Act—would require that online pharmacies fill orders for people who have a prescription written by a doctor who as a "qualifying medical relationship." with the patient. For certain types of drugs, that relationship would mean that the doctor has conducted at least one in-person evaluation. With respect to psychiatric drugs like Prozac—where the patient's demeanor and behavior should be relevant to the doctor's prescription decision—this seems like a very good idea.

If the Act becomes law [which it had not as of May 2009], online pharmacies will also be required to display a statement indicating they are complying with relevant state and federal law, and meet all state-level pharmacy licensing requirements. Penalties for the more serious categories of violations would carry up [to a] maximum sentence of 20 years imprisonment and a fine of up to $2.5 million. One can only hope that these kinds of penalties will prevent what happened to young John McKay from ever repeating itself.

# CHAPTER 4

# Prohibition of Internet Offerings of Child Pornography Is Constitutional

# Case Overview

## *United States v. Williams* (2008)

Congress has made several attempts to solve the problem of child pornography on the Internet, which is very difficult to control in a manner that does not violate citizens' rights to free speech. The Child Pornography Prevention Act (CPPA) of 1996 banned it, but the Supreme Court ruled that the CPPA was unconstitutional. Pornography in general, as distinguished from obscenity, cannot be prohibited because that would violate the First Amendment's guarantee of free speech. Child pornography *can* be—not because of its content, but because the production of it harms the children who take part. The difficulty with the CPPA was that it covered all child pornography, including that not made with real children, such as virtual pornography created with computer graphics. It also could have been applied to movies made with young-looking actors who were actually over eighteen—even *Romeo and Juliet*—which Congress did not intend and which did not qualify for the exception to the First Amendment based on protecting real children. So in 2002 the CPPA was struck down.

After that, Congress tried again and passed the PROTECT (Prosecutorial Remedies and Other Tools to End the Exploitation of Children Today) Act. Its authors realized that given the capabilities of modern computer graphics technology, it would be almost impossible to prove that any image was an actual photograph of real children, and that therefore, no matter how a ban was worded, many pornographers would evade conviction. Therefore, the PROTECT Act focuses not on the actual content of the material, but on the intent of the parties to a transaction. It targets any person who "advertises, promotes, presents, distributes, or solicits through the mails, or in interstate or foreign commerce by any means, including by computer, any material or purported material in a manner that reflects the belief, or that is intended to cause another to believe, that the material or purported material is, or contains . . . a visual depiction of an actual minor engaging in sexually explicit conduct."

In April 2004, Michael Williams, using a sexually explicit screen name, signed in to a public Internet chat room. A secret service agent who had also signed in to the chat room noticed that Williams had posted a message that read: "Dad of toddler has 'good' pics of her an [sic] me for swap of your toddler pics, or live cam." After a conversation with the agent, Williams messaged that he had photographs of men molesting his four-year-old daughter. Eventually, he posted a link leading to seven pictures of actual children, aged approximately five to fifteen, engaging in sexually explicit conduct. The agent then obtained a search warrant for Williams's home, where hard drives containing many more such pictures were seized. Williams was arrested and charged with pandering under the PROTECT Act as well as with possession of child pornography. He pleaded guilty to both but reserved the right to challenge the constitutionality of the PROTECT Act—a challenge that the district court rejected. The court of appeals reversed Williams's pandering conviction, ruling that the PROTECT Act was too broad and too vague. The case then went to the U.S. Supreme Court.

The justices of the Court were divided in their opinions and found the case difficult to resolve. There is a legal convention called the "overbreadth doctrine" under which a defendant's attorneys can challenge a law on the basis not of their client's conduct—which in Williams's case was clearly what the law had been intended to punish—but of hypothetical, imaginary situations in which it might cover someone else's innocent actions. That was what had happened in the CPPA's case, and it was happening in this one. Some of the justices began to question the overbreadth doctrine itself. The majority of them found the suggested hypothetical situations rather far-fetched. In the end, they upheld the law by a vote of seven to two. The dissenters, however, felt strongly that it was wrong to punish anyone on the basis of a belief.

> "The [PROTECT] Act ... does not pro-
> hibit advocacy of child pornography,
> but only offers to provide or requests to
> obtain it. There is no doubt that this
> prohibition falls well within constitu-
> tional bounds."

# Majority Opinion: The PROTECT Act Is Constitutional

*Antonin Scalia*

*Antonin Scalia became a U.S Supreme Court justice in 1986 and as of mid-2009 he is its second most senior member. He is a strong conservative who believes in a strict interpretation of the Constitution, according to the meaning it had when originally adopted. In the following majority opinion in* United States v. Williams, *he argues that the lower court's reasons for declaring the PROTECT Act unconstitutional are not valid. The PRO-TECT Act prohibits offering material that is believed to contain child pornography, or is presented in a way intended to make the recipient believe that it does. It was passed by Congress to re-place a previous law that the Court had struck down because it prohibited possession of material not produced with real chil-dren, which does not fall under the child pornography exception to First Amendment protection of free speech. The new law fo-cuses on the intent of the parties to the transaction rather than the material itself. Its opponents have claimed that it could be applied to innocent transactions involving material that is not actually pornographic, but the Court considers this unlikely to*

Antonin Scalia, majority opinion, *United States v. Williams*, U.S. Supreme Court, May 19, 2008. Reproduced by permission.

*happen; it considers some of the scenarios that have been imag-
ined as "fanciful." For example, the law could not be applied to
Hollywood movies because everyone knows that teen sex scenes
in mainstream movies do not show real sex acts and are made
with young-looking adult actors.*

According to our First Amendment overbreadth doctrine, a
statute is facially invalid if it prohibits a substantial
amount of protected speech. The doctrine seeks to strike a
balance between competing social costs. On the one hand, the
threat of enforcement of an overbroad law deters people from
engaging in constitutionally protected speech, inhibiting the
free exchange of ideas. On the other hand, invalidating a law
that in some of its applications is perfectly constitutional—
particularly a law directed at conduct so antisocial that it has
been made criminal—has obvious harmful effects. . . .

Rather than targeting the underlying material, [the PRO-
TECT Act] bans the collateral speech that introduces such
material into the child-pornography distribution network.
Thus, an Internet user who solicits child pornography from
an undercover agent violates the statute, even if the officer
possesses no child pornography. Likewise, a person who advertises virtual child pornography as depicting actual children
also falls within the reach of the statute. . . .

## Features of the New Law

A number of features of the statute are important to our
analysis:

First, the statute includes a scienter [knowledge of wrong-
doing] requirement. The first word of section 2252A(a)(3)—
"knowingly"—applies to both of the immediately following
subdivisions. . . .

Second, the statute's string of operative verbs—"advertises,
promotes, presents, distributes, or solicits"—is reasonably read
to have a transactional connotation. That is to say, the statute

penalizes speech that accompanies or seeks to induce a transfer of child pornography—via reproduction or physical delivery—from one person to another. . . .

Our conclusion that all the words in this list relate to transactions is not to say that they relate to *commercial* transactions. One could certainly "distribute" child pornography without expecting payment in return. Indeed, in much Internet file sharing of child pornography each participant makes his files available for free to other participants—as Williams did in this case. . . . To run afoul of the statute, the speech need only accompany or seek to induce the transfer of child pornography from one person to another.

Third, the phrase "in a manner that reflects the belief" includes both subjective and objective components. "[A] manner that reflects the belief" is quite different from "a manner that would give one cause to believe." The first formulation suggests that the defendant must actually have held the subjective "belief" that the material or purported material was child pornography. Thus, a misdescription that leads the listener to believe the defendant is offering child pornography, when the defendant in fact does not believe the material is child pornography, does not violate this prong of the statute. (It may, however, violate the "manner . . . that is intended to cause another to believe" prong if the misdescription is intentional.) There is also an objective component to the phrase "manner that reflects the belief." The statement or action must objectively manifest a belief that the material is child pornography; a mere belief, without an accompanying statement or action that would lead a reasonable person to understand that the defendant holds that belief, is insufficient.

Fourth, the other key phrase, "in a manner . . . that is intended to cause another to believe," contains only a subjective element: The defendant must "intend" that the listener believe the material to be child pornography, and must select a manner of "advertising, promoting, presenting, distributing, or soliciting" the material that *he* thinks will engender that belief—whether or not a reasonable person would think the same.

Fifth, the definition of "sexually explicit conduct" (the visual depiction of which, engaged in by an actual minor, is covered by the Act's pandering and soliciting prohibition even when it is not obscene) . . . connotes actual depiction of the sex act rather than merely the suggestion that it is occurring. And "simulated" sexual intercourse is not sexual intercourse that is merely suggested, but rather sexual intercourse that is explicitly portrayed, even though (through camera tricks or otherwise) it may not actually have occurred. The portrayal must cause a reasonable viewer to believe that the actors actually engaged in that conduct on camera. Critically, unlike in *Free Speech Coalition's* requirement of a "visual depiction of an actual minor" makes clear that, although the sexual intercourse may be simulated, it must involve actual children (unless it is obscene). This change eliminates any possibility that virtual child pornography or sex between youthful-looking adult actors might be covered by the term "simulated sexual intercourse."

## No Protection of Illegal Offers

We now turn to whether the statute, as we have construed it, criminalizes a substantial amount of protected expressive activity.

Offers to engage in illegal transactions are categorically excluded from First Amendment protection. One would think that this principle resolves the present case, since the statute criminalizes only offers to provide or requests to obtain contraband—child obscenity and child pornography involving actual children, both of which are proscribed, and the proscription of which is constitutional. The Eleventh Circuit, however, believed that the exclusion of First Amendment protection extended only to *commercial* offers to provide or receive contraband. . . .

This mistakes the rationale for the categorical exclusion. It is based not on the less privileged First Amendment status of commercial speech, but on the principle that offers to give or receive what it is unlawful to possess, have no social value and thus, like obscenity, enjoy no First Amendment protection. Many long established criminal proscriptions—such as laws against conspiracy, incitement, and solicitation—criminalize speech (commercial or not) that is intended to induce or commence illegal activities. Offers to provide or requests to obtain unlawful material, whether as part of a commercial exchange or not, are similarly undeserving of First Amendment protection. It would be an odd constitutional principle that permitted the government to prohibit offers to sell illegal drugs, but not offers to give them away for free.

To be sure, there remains an important distinction between a proposal to engage in illegal activity and the abstract advocacy of illegality. The Act before us does not prohibit advocacy of child pornography, but only offers to provide or requests to obtain it. There is no doubt that this prohibition falls well within constitutional bounds. The constitutional defect we found in the pandering provision at issue in *Free Speech Coalition* was that it went *beyond* pandering to prohibit possession of material that could not otherwise be proscribed.

In sum, we hold that offers to provide or requests to obtain child pornography are categorically excluded from the First Amendment. . . .

The Eleventh Circuit believed it a constitutional difficulty that no child pornography need exist to trigger the statute. In its view, the fact that the statute could punish a "braggart, exaggerator, or outright liar" rendered it unconstitutional. That seems to us a strange constitutional calculus. Although we have held that the government can ban *both* fraudulent offers, *and* offers to provide illegal products, the Eleventh Circuit would forbid the government from punishing *fraudulent offers to provide illegal products.* We see no logic in that position; if anything, such statements are doubly excluded from the First Amendment. . . .

The Eleventh Circuit found "particularly objectionable" the fact that the "reflects the belief" prong of the statute could ensnare a person who mistakenly believes that material is child pornography. This objection has two conceptually distinct parts. First, the Eleventh Circuit thought that it would be unconstitutional to punish someone for mistakenly distributing virtual child pornography as real child pornography. We disagree. Offers to deal in illegal products or otherwise engage in illegal activity do not acquire First Amendment protection when the offeror is mistaken about the factual predicate of his offer. The pandering and solicitation made unlawful by the Act are sorts of inchoate crimes—acts looking toward the commission of another crime, the delivery of child pornography. As with other inchoate crimes—attempt and conspiracy, for example—impossibility of completing the crime because the facts were not as the defendant believed is not a defense. . . .

## Nonpornographic Material Excluded

The Eleventh Circuit also thought that the statute could apply to someone who subjectively believes that an innocuous picture of a child is "lascivious." (Clause (v) of the definition of "sexually explicit conduct" is "lascivious exhibition of the genitals or pubic area of any person.") That is not so. The defendant must believe that the picture contains certain material, and that material in fact (and not merely in his estimation) must meet the statutory definition. Where the material at issue is a harmless picture of a child in a bathtub and the defendant, knowing that material, erroneously believes that it constitutes a "lascivious display of the genitals," the statute has no application.

Williams and *amici* [friends of the court] raise other objections, which demonstrate nothing so forcefully as the tendency of our overbreadth doctrine to summon forth an endless stream of fanciful hypotheticals. Williams argues, for example, that a person who offers nonpornographic photographs of young girls to a pedophile could be punished under the statute if the pedophile secretly expects that the pictures will contain child pornography. That hypothetical does not implicate the statute, because the offeror does not hold the belief or intend the recipient to believe that the material is child pornography.

*Amici* contend that some advertisements for mainstream Hollywood movies that depict underage characters having sex violate the statute. We think it implausible that a reputable distributor of Hollywood movies, such as Amazon.com, believes that one of these films contains *actual* children engaging in *actual or simulated* sex on camera; and even more implausible that Amazon.com would *intend* to make its customers believe such a thing. The average person understands that sex scenes in mainstream movies use nonchild actors, depict sexual activity in a way that would not rise to the explicit level necessary under the statute, or, in most cases, both.

There was raised at oral argument the question whether turning child pornography over to the police might not count as "present[ing]" the material. An interpretation of "presents" that would include turning material over to the authorities would of course be self-defeating in a statute that looks to the prosecution of people who deal in child pornography. . . .

It was also suggested at oral argument that the statute might cover documentary footage of atrocities being committed in foreign countries, such as soldiers raping young children. Perhaps so, if the material rises to the high level of explicitness that we have held is required. That sort of documentary footage could of course be the subject of an as-applied challenge. The courts presumably would weigh the educational interest in the dissemination of information about the atrocities against the government's interest in preventing the distribution of materials that constitute "a permanent record" of the children's degradation whose dissemination increases "the harm to the child." Assuming that the constitutional balance would have to be struck in favor of the documentary, the existence of that exception would not establish that the statute is *substantially* overbroad. The "mere fact that one can conceive of some impermissible applications of a statute is not sufficient to render it susceptible to an overbreadth challenge." *Members of City Council of Los Angeles v. Taxpayers of Vincent*. In the vast majority of its applications, this statute raises no constitutional problems whatever.

## The Law Does Not Prohibit Virtual Pornography

Finally, the dissent accuses us of silently overruling our prior decisions in *New York v. Ferber* and *Free Speech Coalition*. According to the dissent, Congress has made an end-run around the First Amendment's protection of virtual child pornography by prohibiting proposals to transact in such images rather than prohibiting the images themselves. But an offer to provide or request to receive virtual child pornography is not prohibited by the statute. A crime is committed only when the speaker believes or intends the listener to believe that the subject of the proposed transaction depicts *real* children. It is simply not true that this means "a protected category of expression [will] inevitably be suppressed". Simulated child pornography will be as available as ever, so long as it is offered and sought *as such* and not as real child pornography. The dissent would require an exception from the statute's prohibition when, unbeknownst to one or both of the parties to the proposal, the completed transaction would not have been unlawful because it is (we have said) protected by the First Amendment. We fail to see what First Amendment interest would be served by drawing a distinction between two defendants who attempt to acquire contraband, one of whom happens to be mistaken about the contraband nature of what he would acquire. Is Congress forbidden from punishing those who attempt to acquire what they believe to be national-security documents, but which are actually fakes? To ask is to answer. There is no First Amendment exception from the general principle of criminal law that a person attempting to commit a crime need not be exonerated because he has a mistaken view of the facts. . . .

The Eleventh Circuit believed that the phrases "'in a manner that reflects the belief'" and "'in a manner . . . that is intended to cause another to believe'" are "so vague and standardless as to what may not be said that the public is left with no objective measure to which behavior can be conformed." The court gave two examples. First, an email claiming to contain photograph attachments and including a message that says "'little Janie in the bath—hubba, hubba!'" According to the Eleventh Circuit, given that the statute does not require the actual existence of illegal material, the Government would have "virtually unbounded discretion" to deem such a statement in violation of the "'reflects the belief'" prong. The court's second example was an e-mail entitled "'Good pics of kids in bed'" with a photograph attachment of toddlers in pajamas asleep in their beds. The court described three hypothetical senders: a proud grandparent, a "chronic forwarder of cute photos with racy tongue-in-cheek subject lines," and a child molester who seeks to trade the photographs for more graphic material. According to the Eleventh Circuit, because the "manner" in which the photographs are sent is the same in each case, and because the identity of the sender and the content of the photographs are irrelevant under the statute, all three senders could arguably be prosecuted for pandering.

We think that neither of these hypotheticals, without further facts, would enable a reasonable juror to find, beyond a reasonable doubt, that the speaker believed and spoke in a manner that reflected the belief, or spoke in a manner intended to cause another to believe, that the pictures displayed actual children engaged in "sexually explicit conduct" as defined in the Act. The prosecutions would be thrown out at the threshold.

But the Eleventh Circuit's error is more fundamental than merely its selection of unproblematic hypotheticals. Its basic mistake lies in the belief that the mere fact that close cases can be envisioned renders a statute vague. That is not so. Close cases can be imagined under virtually any statute. The problem that poses is addressed, not by the doctrine of vagueness, but by the requirement of proof beyond a reasonable doubt....

Child pornography harms and debases the most defenseless of our citizens. Both the State and Federal Governments have sought to suppress it for many years, only to find it proliferating through the new medium of the Internet. This Court held unconstitutional Congress's previous attempt to meet this new threat, and Congress responded with a carefully crafted attempt to eliminate the First Amendment problems we identified. As far as the provision at issue in this case is concerned, that effort was successful.

> "Without some demonstration that ju-
> ries have been rendering exploitation of
> children unpunishable, there is no ex-
> cuse for cutting back on the First
> Amendment. . . . I would hold [the
> PROTECT Act] unconstitutional."

# Dissenting Opinion:
# The PROTECT Act Violates
# the First Amendment

*David Souter*

*David Souter became a Supreme Court justice in 1990. Although
he was thought to be a conservative when appointed, he has often voted with the Court's liberal wing. In the following dissenting opinion in* United States v. Williams, *in which he was joined
by Justice Ruth Bader Ginsburg, he states that he does not agree
with the Court's ruling that the PROTECT Act is constitutional.
The act prohibits offering or soliciting material that is believed
to contain child pornography produced with real children. It is
true, he asserts, that transactions involving illegal material are
not covered by the First Amendment guarantee of free speech.
But under this law, a person can be punished for offering photos
that were not made with real children, simply for leading someone to believe they were. As virtual or faked pornographic photos
are not illegal, the rule that a mere attempt to commit a crime is
punishable does not apply; there would be no crime if the transaction were completed. Upholding this law, Souter argues, would
wipe out the Court's decisions in earlier child pornography cases*

David Souter, dissenting opinion, *United States v. Williams*, U.S. Supreme Court, May
19, 2008. Reproduced by permission.

*just as surely as if they had been formally overruled, and that should not be done without a better reason than he believes exists.*

Dealing in obscenity is penalized without violating the First Amendment, but as a general matter pornography lacks the harm to justify prohibiting it. If, however, a photograph (to take the kind of image in this case) shows an actual minor child as a pornographic subject, its transfer and even its possession may be made criminal. The exception to the general rule rests not on the content of the picture but on the need to foil the exploitation of child subjects, and the justification limits the exception: only pornographic photographs of actual children may be prohibited. Thus, just six years ago [in 2002] the Court struck down a statute outlawing particular material merely represented to be child pornography, but not necessarily depicting actual children.

The Prosecutorial Remedies and Other Tools to end the Exploitation of Children Today [PROTECT] Act of 2003 (Act), was enacted in the wake of *Ashcroft v. Free Speech Coalition*. The Act responds by avoiding any direct prohibition of transactions in child pornography when no actual minors may be pictured; instead, it prohibits proposals for transactions in pornography when a defendant manifestly believes or would induce belief in a prospective party that the subject of an exchange or exhibition is or will be an actual child, not an impersonated, simulated or "virtual" one, or the subject of a composite created from lawful photos spliced together. . . .

The Court holds it is constitutional to prohibit these proposals, and up to a point I do not disagree. In particular, I accept the Court's explanation that Congress may criminalize proposals unrelated to any extant [actually existing] image. I part ways from the Court, however, on the regulation of proposals made with regard to specific, existing representations. Under the new law, the elements of the pandering offense are the same, whether or not the images are of real children. As to those that do not show real children, of course, a transaction in the material could not be prosecuted consistently with the First Amendment, and I believe that maintaining the First Amendment protection of expression we have previously held to cover fake child pornography requires a limit to the law's criminalization of pandering proposals. In failing to confront the tension between ostensibly protecting the material pandered while approving prosecution of the pandering of that same material, and in allowing the new pandering prohibition to suppress otherwise protected speech, the Court undermines *New York v. Ferber* and *Free Speech Coalition* in both reasoning and result. This is the significant element of today's holding, and I respectfully dissent from it.

## Punishes Offers of Legal Photos

The easy case for applying the Act would be a proposal to obtain or supply child pornography supposedly showing a real child, when the solicitation or offer is unrelated to any image (that is, when the existence of pornographic "material" was merely "purported"). A proposal speaking of a pornographic photograph of a child is (absent any disclaimer or qualification) understood to mean a photo of an actual child; the reasonable assumption is that people desiring child pornography are not looking for fake child pornography, so that those who speak about it mean the real thing. Hence, someone who seeks to obtain child pornography (having no specific artifact in mind) "solicits" an unlawful transfer of contraband. On the other side of that sort of proposed transaction, someone with nothing to supply or having only non-expressive matter who purports to present, distribute, advertise, or promote child pornography also proposes an illegal transaction. In both cases, the activity would amount to an offer to traffic in child pornography that may be suppressed, and the First Amendment does not categorically protect offers to engage in illegal transactions. To the extent the speaker intended to mislead others, a conviction would also square with the unprotected status of fraud, and even a non-fraudulent speaker who mistakenly believed he could obtain the forbidden contraband to transfer to anyone who accepted an offer could be validly convicted consistent with the general rule of criminal law, that attempting to commit a crime is punishable even though the completed crime might (or would) turn out to be impossible in fact.

The easy cases for constitutional application of the Act are over, however, when one gets to proposals for transactions related to extant pornographic objects, like photos in a dealer's inventory, for example. These will in fact be the common cases, as the legislative findings attest. Congress did not pass the Act to catch unsuccessful solicitors or fraudulent offerors with no photos to sell; rather, it feared that "[t]he mere prospect that the technology exists to create composite or computer-generated depictions that are indistinguishable from depictions of real children will allow defendants who possess images of real children to escape prosecution. . . . This threatens to render child pornography laws that protect real children unenforceable."

A person who "knowingly" proposes a transaction in an extant image incorporates into the proposal an understanding that the subject of the proposal is or includes that image. Congress understood that underlying most proposals there will be an image that shows a child, and the proposal referring to an actual child's picture will thus amount to a proposal to commit an independent crime such as a transfer of child pornography. But even when actual pictures thus occasion proposals, the Act requires no finding that an actual child be shown in the pornographic setting in order to prove a violation. And the fair assumption (apparently made by Congress) is that in some instances, the child pornography in question will be fake, with the picture showing only a simulation of a child, for example, or a very young-looking adult convincingly passed off as a child; in those cases the proposal is for a transaction that could not itself be made criminal, because the absence of a child model means that the image is constitutionally protected. But under the Act, that is irrelevant. What matters is not the inclusion of an actual child in the image, or the validity of forbidding the transaction proposed; what counts is simply the manifest belief or intent to cause a belief that a true minor is shown in the pornographic depiction referred to.

The tension with existing constitutional law is obvious. *Free Speech Coalition* reaffirmed that non-obscene virtual pornographic images are protected, because they fail to trigger the concern for child safety that disentitles child pornography to First Amendment protection. . . . The Act, however, punishes proposals regarding images when the inclusion of actual children is not established by the prosecution, as well as images that show no real children at all; and this, despite the fact that, under *Free Speech Coalition*, the first proposed transfer could not be punished without the very proof the Act is meant to dispense with, and the second could not be made criminal at all.

## Problem Unresolved by the Court

What justification can there be for making independent crimes of proposals to engage in transactions that may include protected materials? The Court gives three answers, none of which comes to grips with the difficulty raised by the question. The first, says it is simply wrong to say that the Act makes it criminal to propose a lawful transaction, since an element of the forbidden proposal must express a belief or inducement to believe that the subject of the proposed transaction shows actual children. But this does not go to the point. The objection is not that the Act criminalizes a proposal for a transaction described as being in virtual (that is, protected) child pornography. The point is that some proposals made criminal, because they express a belief that they refer to real child pornography, will relate to extant material that does not, or cannot be, demonstrated to show real children and so may not be prohibited. When a proposal covers existing photographs, the Act does not require that the requisite belief (manifested or encouraged) in the reality of the subjects be a correct belief. Prohibited proposals may relate to transactions in lawful, as well as unlawful, pornography.

Much the same may be said about the Court's second answer, that a proposal to commit a crime enjoys no speech protection. For the reason just given, that answer does not face up to the source of the difficulty: the action actually contemplated in the proposal, the transfer of the particular image, is not criminal if it turns out that an actual child is not shown in the photograph. . . . It is not enough just to say that the First Amendment does not protect proposals to commit crimes. For that rule rests on the assumption that the proposal is actually to commit a crime, not to do an act that may turn out to be no crime at all. Why should the general rule of unprotected criminal proposals cover a case like the proposal to transfer what may turn out to be fake child pornography?

The Court's third answer analogizes the proposal to an attempt to commit a crime, and relies on the rule of criminal law that an attempt is criminal even when some impediment makes it impossible to complete the criminal act (the possible impediment here being the advanced age, say, or simulated character of the child-figure). Although the actual transfer the speaker has in mind may not turn out to be criminal, the argument goes, the transfer intended by the speaker is criminal, because the speaker believes that the contemplated transfer will be of real child pornography, and transfer of real child pornography is criminal. The fact that the circumstances are not as he believes them to be, because the material does not depict actual minors, is no defense to his attempt to engage in an unlawful transaction. . . .

The more serious failure of the attempt analogy, however, is its unjustifiable extension of the classic factual frustration rule, under which the action specifically intended would be a criminal act if completed. The intending killer who mistakenly grabs the pistol loaded with blanks would have committed homicide if bullets had been in the gun; it was only the impossibility of completing the very intended act of shooting bullets that prevented the completion of the crime. This is not so, however, in the proposed transaction in an identified pornographic image without the showing of a real child; no matter what the parties believe, and no matter how exactly a defendant's actions conform to his intended course of conduct in completing the transaction he has in mind, if there turns out to be reasonable doubt that a real child was used to make the photos, or none was, there could be, respectively, no conviction and no crime. . . .

## Invalid Analogies with Other Crimes

The Court's first response is to demur, with its example of the drug dealer who sells something else. (A package of baking powder, not powder cocaine, would be an example.) No one doubts the dealer may validly be convicted of an attempted drug sale even if he didn't know it was baking powder he was selling. Yet selling baking powder is no more criminal than selling virtual child pornography.

This response does not suffice, however, because it overlooks a difference between the lawfulness of selling baking powder and the lawful character of virtual child pornography. Powder sales are lawful but not constitutionally privileged. Any justification within the bounds of rationality would suffice for limiting baking powder transactions, just as it would for regulating the discharge of blanks from a pistol. Virtual pornography, however, has been held to fall within the First Amendment speech privilege, and thus is affirmatively protected, not merely allowed as a matter of course. The question stands: why should a proposal that may turn out to cover privileged expression be subject to standard attempt liability?

The Court's next response deals with the privileged character of the underlying material. It gives another example of attempt that presumably could be made criminal, in the case of the mistaken spy, who passes national security documents thinking they are classified and secret, when in fact they have been declassified and made subject to public inspection. Publishing unclassified documents is subject to the First Amendment privilege and can claim a value that fake child pornography cannot. The Court assumes that the document publication may be punished as an attempt to violate state-secret restrictions (and I assume so too); then why not attempt-proposals based on a mistaken belief that the underlying material is real child pornography? As the Court looks at it, the deterrent value that justifies prosecuting the mistaken spy (like the mistaken drug dealer and the intending killer) would presumably validate prosecuting those who make proposals about fake child pornography. But it would not, for there are significant differences between the cases of security documents and pornography without real children.

Where Government documents, blank cartridges, and baking powder are involved, deterrence can be promoted without compromising any other important policy, which is not true of criminalizing mistaken child pornography proposals. There are three dispositive differences. As for the first, if the law can criminalize proposals for transactions in fake as well as true child pornography as if they were like attempts to sell cocaine that turned out to be baking powder, constitutional law will lose something sufficiently important to have made it into multiple holdings of this Court, and that is the line between child pornography that may be suppressed and fake child pornography that falls within First Amendment protection. No one can seriously assume that after today's decision the Government will go on prosecuting defendants for selling child pornography (requiring a showing that a real child is pictured, under *Free Speech Coalition*); it will prosecute for merely proposing a pornography transaction manifesting or inducing the belief that a photo is real child pornography, free of any need to demonstrate that any extant underlying photo does show a real child. If the Act can be enforced, it will function just as it was meant to do, by merging the whole subject of child pornography into the offense of proposing a transaction, dispensing with the real-child element in the underlying subject. And eliminating the need to prove a real child will be a loss of some consequence. This is so not because there will possibly be less pornography available owing to the greater ease of prosecuting, but simply because there must be a line between what the Government may suppress and what it may not, and a segment of that line will be gone. This Court went to great pains to draw it in *Ferber* and *Free Speech Coalition*; it was worth drawing and it is worth respecting now in facing the attempt to end-run that line through the provisions of the Act.

## The Act Eliminates a Class of Protected Speech

The second reason for treating child pornography differently follows from the first. If the deluded drug dealer is held liable for an attempted crime there is no risk of eliminating baking powder from trade in lawful commodities. Likewise, if the mistaken spy is convicted of attempting to disclose classified national security documents there will be no worry that lawful speech will be suppressed as a consequence; any unclassified documents in question can be quoted in the newspaper, other unclassified documents will circulate, and analysts of politics and foreign policy will be able to rely on them. But if the Act can effectively eliminate the real-child requirement when a proposal relates to extant material, a class of protected speech will disappear. True, what will be lost is short on merit, but intrinsic value is not the reason for protecting unpopular expression.

Finally, if the Act stands when applied to identifiable, extant pornographic photographs, then in practical terms *Ferber* and *Free Speech Coalition* fall. They are left as empty as if the Court overruled them formally, and when a case as well considered and as recently decided as *Free Speech Coalition* is put aside (after a mere six years) there ought to be a very good reason. . . . Attempts with baking powder and unclassified documents can be punished without damage to confidence in precedent; suppressing protected pornography cannot be.

These differences should be dispositive. Eliminating the line between protected and unprotected speech, guaranteeing the suppression of a category of expression previously protected, and reducing recent and carefully considered First Amendment precedents to empty shells are heavy prices, not to be paid without a substantial offset, which is missing from this case. Hence, my answer that there is no justification for saving the Act's attempt to get around our holdings. We should hold that a transaction in what turns out to be fake pornography is better understood, not as an incomplete attempt to commit a crime, but as a completed series of intended acts that simply do not add up to a crime, owing to the privileged character of the material the parties were in fact about to deal in. . . .

Untethering the power to suppress proposals about extant pornography from any assessment of the likely effects the proposals might have has an unsettling significance well beyond the subject of child pornography. For the Court is going against the grain of pervasive First Amendment doctrine that tolerates speech restriction not on mere general tendencies of expression, or the private understandings of speakers or listeners, but only after a critical assessment of practical consequences. . . .

*Brandenburg v. Ohio* insists that any limit on speech be grounded in a realistic, factual assessment of harm. This is a far cry from the Act before us now, which rests criminal prosecution for proposing transactions in expressive material on nothing more than a speaker's statement about the material itself, a statement that may disclose no more than his own belief about the subjects represented or his desire to foster belief in another. This should weigh heavily in the overbreadth balance, because "First Amendment freedoms are most in danger when the government seeks to control thought or to justify its laws for that impermissible end. The right to think is the beginning of freedom, and speech must be protected from the government because speech is the beginning of thought." *Free Speech Coalition.* . . .

## Act Not Needed to Prosecute

I said that I would not pay the price enacted by the Act without a substantial justification, which I am at a loss to find here. I have to assume that the Court sees some grounding for the Act that I do not, however, and I suppose the holding can only be explained as an uncritical acceptance of a claim made both to Congress and to this Court. In each forum the Government argued that a jury's appreciation of the mere possibility of simulated or virtual child pornography will prevent convictions for the real thing, by inevitably raising reasonable doubt about whether actual children are shown. . . .

Perhaps I am wrong, but without some demonstration that juries have been rendering exploitation of children unpunishable, there is no excuse for cutting back on the First Amendment and no alternative to finding overbreadth in this Act. I would hold it unconstitutional.

*"The Justices . . . went so far . . . as to suggest they may want to curtail the First Amendment in order to save the law."*

# The PROTECT Act May Be the First Law Against Internet Porn to Be Upheld

## Lyle Denniston

*Lyle Denniston is a journalist who has covered the Supreme Court for nearly fifty years. In the following article he describes the Supreme Court's public hearing in* United States v. Williams, *relating some of the oral arguments of the attorneys and what the justices said about them. The case concerned the PROTECT Act, a new law against child pornography that Congress had passed hoping that it would not be judged unconstitutional, as previous anti–child porn laws had been. The chief problem with such laws, asserts Denniston, is that sometimes their wording, in the attempt to prohibit pornography, unintentionally covers material that is protected as free speech by the First Amendment to the Constitution. When this happens, the law is considered "too broad" and is struck down. The principle that an accused person can challenge the constitutionality of a law by claiming that it is too broad, even if his or her own activity is unquestionably what the law was intended to prohibit, is called the "overbreadth doctrine." In this case, Denniston contends, the justices began to wonder whether the overbreadth doctrine should be set aside. They were worried about the spread of child por-*

Lyle Denniston, "Commentary: An Anti-Porn Law that Will Survive?" *SCOTUS Blog*, October 30, 2007. Reproduced by permission of the author.

*nography on the Internet, yet it might be impossible to word an antiporn law in such a way that no protected expression could conceivably be covered by it.*

Driven by an obvious worry that child pornography is spreading rapidly on the Internet, and seeming to sense that some day, somehow they should uphold a law to deal with it, Supreme Court Justices did some public brainstorming [October 30, 2007,] about how to write an opinion that would do just that. After spending about 20 minutes musing over hypotheticals [imaginary cases] that might suggest Congress went too far in 2003 in writing a new criminal law against Internet pornography that depicts real or computer-drawn children engaging in sex acts, the Justices then turned about and went so far in the other direction as to suggest they may want to curtail the First Amendment in order to save the law. Some of them actually toyed with the idea of casting aside the long-standing doctrine that an individual who may well have violated a law governing expression should be able to complain that it is unconstitutional because it might inhibit someone else's free speech—the "overbreadth doctrine."

This was the decidedly two-sided shape of the hearing on *United States v. Williams*—an indication that it could take months of deliberation before the Court decides which way to go in the final ruling. Illustrating the cross-currents during the one-hour session, Solicitor General Paul D. Clement appeared to be beleaguered during the first portion, reaching for conciliatory suggestions as to how the law might be understood to have less sweep, while his adversary, Coral Gables, Fla., attorney Richard J. Diaz, was pressured unrelentingly in the second half, leading him to concede that maybe the law—though still problematic—did not reach as far as he had complained. It was not as if the Justices were being even-handed; rather, they sounded as if they were warming to the law's validity the longer they talked about it.

# The PROTECT Act

The case addresses the latest attempt by Congress—several times frustrated by past defeats in court on the issue—to pass a child porn law that might survive constitutional scrutiny even though it might reach some expression that otherwise would be shielded by the First Amendment. This version goes by the name "PROTECT Act"—short for "Prosecutorial Remedies and Other Tools to End the Exploitation of Children Today Act." It was enacted [in 2003], one year after the Supreme Court had struck down a 1996 version.

The new law criminalized pandering in child pornography, barring the promotion, presentation, distribution or solicitation of any material that is shown in a way to reflect the belief—or cause someone else to believe—that the actual or purported material does contain child pornography, even if it actually does not. Convicted under the law, Floridian Michael Williams was caught—in an undercover operation—offering on the Internet sexually explicit images of him and his daughter, and other images of children engaging in sex acts. He was sentenced to five years in prison. The Eleventh Circuit struck down the pandering part of his conviction, finding that that part of the PROTECT Act violated the First Amendment because it was overbroad and vague. The government has appealed, seeking to revive those clauses.

While the Solicitor General was at the podium, the Justices explored an array of hypotheticals, testing him on the law's potential impact on movie critics—perhaps reviewing *Lolita*, makers or distributors of documentaries or newsreels that show the rape of children in a war zone, public school pupils trading "dirty pictures" and asking to see more, or householders who received child porn unsolicited in the mail and either told neighbors or the police about it.

After posing some of those scenarios, the Justices seemed incredulous that the PROTECT Act might cover them. Justice Stephen G. Breyer, for example, who mentioned the school students' exchange of "dirty pictures," told Clement that his broad view of the Act, would "criminalize activity in school, and all over he place." Breyer—joined by Chief Justice John G. Roberts, Jr.—said that the government's brief had seemed to outline a narrower scope for the law than Clement was now offering. Justice Anthony M. Kennedy also wondered if there were anything in the language of the law, as Clement read it, that would limit the scope of the kind of promotional activity that would be criminalized.

To each one of the hypotheticals put before him, the Solicitor General argued that the Act would not apply—or, if it did, the claimed innocence of the activity could be used as a defense to an actual criminal prosecution. His heavy reliance upon the prospect of "as-applied" challenges as the way to curb any excessive reach of the law did not seem to mollify most of the Justices. (It was clear, from the remarks of Justices Antonin Scalia and Samuel A. Alito, Jr., that Clement and the law had their full support, and thus they joined efforts in trying to counter the negative reaction of some on the bench.)

## Defining Exclusions from the Law

After a time, Clement was putting emphasis on ways that the Court could interpret the law by reading its provisions in a more confined way, and emphasizing that violations of the law had to be based upon proof of both an objective test—a reasonable person test of what the law reached—and a subjective test—what the accused individual had intended about pandering or promoting child porn.

Williams' lawyer, Diaz, opened with a fervent argument that the PROTECT Act would sweep so widely that it "punishes thought, belief and opinion," and reaches even "materials that may not, in fact, exist" because someone offering or soliciting such materials could be prosecuted for trying to promote a fictitious depiction as if it were the real thing.

Soon, his argument was interrupted by a comment by Breyer, noting that the Solicitor General had countered every example cited in Diaz's brief of the potential coverage of the law, refuting each claim that protected expression would be grasped by the Act. As it turned out, Breyer was actually beginning an exploration of how to craft an opinion that would list all the hypotheticals that the law does not cover, in order to uphold it as being narrowly confined. (Breyer, of course, insisted he was not committing himself or the Court to any particular opinion.)

Before that process resumed, Diaz was given a lecture by Justice Scalia about how and why the First Amendment's free speech protection does not embrace lying—his response to the lawyer's argument that the Act would criminalize mere lying about what was in offered Internet material, by misrepresenting it as the real thing. He also was pressed, somewhat testily, by Justice Alito to come up with convincing examples to show that the law was overbroad in its reach.

After that exchange, Breyer outlined the opinion-writing approach he was thinking about. It would have an appendix listing the hypotheticals of expression that the law was claimed to reach, with the Solicitor General's refutation that any would, in fact, be covered in actual prosecutions. It would suggest that the Court had found no examples of excessive breadth, Breyer suggested. Diaz said "That could be done," and it would perhaps constitute "an affirmative defense." But, he said, the list could not encompass every possible scenario, there would be other expression "you hadn't thought of," so some utterances would still be "chilled."

## Reconsidering the Overbreadth Doctrine

Justice Kennedy stepped in, suggesting that "maybe it would be prudent to re-examine our overbreadth doctrine." In this case, Kennedy said, the accused individual "knew what it was" that he was offering "and expressed that belief," so maybe he should not be allowed to make the argument that the law would reach the expression of others. "You could do that," Diaz said, "but it would mean carving another area of speech out of the First Amendment." Chief Justice Roberts immediately disagreed, saying it would not be carving out anything, but would simply be indicating that Williams could not rely on the impact on other people.

By this point, Diaz was appearing to be more willing to concede that the law could be interpreted so that it "would be more narrowly tailored," although he continued to insist it would go on having a chilling effect on "freedom of thought."

Justice David H. Souter picked up on Breyer's notion of how to write an opinion, and said that, while "somewhere out there" the law might have an impact beyond the examples that were said not to be covered, those would not be sufficient to show "substantial overbreadth." "That could be," Diaz replied.

Justice Ruth Bader Ginsburg, who appeared to be the most skeptical about the PROTECT Act, ridiculed Breyer's idea of spelling out the meaning of the law through an appendix listing what it did not cover. That, she said, would be rewriting the law, and the Court had not previously used an appendix to an opinion to spell out a law's meaning. Justice Scalia chimed in that such an appendix would be "blatant dictum," and used his response to suggest that the overbreadth doctrine itself rested upon dicta [comments in a ruling that are not part of the legal basis for the decision]—an implication that it should not be regarded any longer as binding.

Souter tried to come to Breyer's rescue, suggesting that a list of examples excluded from coverage could be written into the body of an opinion, as part of the legal rationale to show that the law did not have "substantial overbreadth."

Kennedy returned to speculation about what to do with overbreadth doctrine during the Solicitor General's brief rebuttal. He wondered if the Court could reject the doctrine in cases like this one, but retain it for other cases.

Clement replied that he was not making an assault on the doctrine, but noted that the burden is on the challenger of a law to prove "substantial overbreadth," emphasizing the word "substantial." Justice Ginsburg had the last word on the subject, noting that the Court had often relied upon the doctrine in First Amendment cases—implying that it would be a considerable step to "toss [it] out."

> "The Supreme Court has upheld a federal law that prohibits pandering child pornography. Doing so, the court restores a measure of common sense to its perplexing obscenity jurisprudence."

# The *Williams* Decision Was Sensible

*National Review Online*

*The following editorial from* National Review Online, *commenting on the Supreme Court's decision in* United States v. Williams, *explains why past laws against child pornography on the Internet were struck down as unconstitutional and expresses relief that one has finally been upheld. In the authors' opinion, the views of past Courts did not reflect those of lawmakers and the communities they represented. When Congress tried again to ban child pornography, lawsuits again were filed claiming that the law was too broad and would suppress legitimate movies depicting teen sex, such as* Romeo and Juliet. *But this time, the Court ruled that when a law is challenged on "overbreadth" grounds its critics must demonstrate that a significant amount of expression protected by the First Amendment will actually be threatened, not merely that a situation can be imagined where it might be. This is as it should be, say the authors. The law will be applied against real offenders, and if anyone ever attempts to misapply it, it can be challenged only with respect to its use in that particular case.*

*National Review Online,* "Supremely Sensible," May 22, 2008. Copyright © 2008 by National Review, Inc., 215 Lexington Avenue, New York, NY 10016. Reproduced by permission.

In a refreshingly lopsided 7-2 ruling, the Supreme Court has upheld a federal law that prohibits pandering child pornography. Doing so, the court restores a measure of common sense to its perplexing obscenity jurisprudence.

On the surface, no First Amendment protection is extended to "sexually explicit material that violates fundamental notions of decency," the Court's standing definition of obscene "speech." Fundamental notions of decency have withered in the last half century, however, and with them the court's capacity to specify the permissible sphere of regulation.

Convinced in 1964 that free-speech principles rendered only "hardcore pornography" subject to proscription, Justice Potter Stewart famously pronounced himself unable to define it to any more rigorous standard than, "I know it when I see it." Under such inscrutable guidelines, a struggle has ensued between lawmakers, whose restrictions on obscenity reflect the values of their communities, and jurists, whose rejections of those restrictions reflect elite, evolving notions of "redeeming social value."

One might have thought common ground could be found on the narrow and revolting matter of child pornography. Such images depict the sexual abuse of minors incapable of consent. The abuse, moreover, feeds on itself, fueled by an underground market that craves nothing so much as new images. But banning traffic in even this condemnable depravity has proved difficult.

In 1996, addressing the explosion of child pornography on the Internet, Congress attempted to criminalize visual depictions of what were, or appeared to be, minors "engaging in sexually explicit conduct." But in *Ashcroft v. Free Speech Coalition* (2002), the Supreme Court invalidated the law. The justices fretted that a provision clearly designed to protect children from exploitation might somehow suppress adaptations of *Romeo and Juliet* and chill what they, in their wisdom, took to be the fundamental right to traffic in "virtual" child pornography.

After *Free Speech Coalition*, the Court's precedents appeared to leave two categories of images subject to preclusion: images of actual children engaging in sex acts, and those of children (actual, virtual, or adults posing as children) engaging in conduct sufficiently lewd to be deemed obscene.

## Challenge by Critics

Congress tried to dry up the market by prohibiting offers or solicitations to exchange such content in interstate and foreign commerce (which of course includes the Internet). As night follows day, the usual suspects filed lawsuits complaining that these carefully targeted proscriptions—in what was, in the current fashion, torturously named the "Prosecutorial Remedies and Other Tools to end the Exploitation of Children Today [PROTECT] Act of 2003"—were too sweeping. Sen. Patrick Leahy, then the ranking member of the Judiciary Committee protested that the law went too far. The Eleventh Circuit federal appeals court agreed.

[The May 22, 2008,] ruling in *United States v Williams* reversed the appellate court and upheld the law. Justice Scalia explained that when a ban on child pornography is challenged on "overbreadth" grounds, complainants must demonstrate not merely that they can come up with some clever *Romeo and Juliet*–type example of a chilling effect; they must instead show that a disproportionate amount of protected speech could realistically be imperiled in the legitimate effort to bar antisocial expression that lies outside the First Amendment's carapace. In this case, the new law took pains to laser in on depravity that clearly enjoys no First Amendment protection. The Court concluded that this law would not be overturned based on speculation about its potential to discourage real art.

This is exactly as it should be. The government can be expected to apply the law, day in and day out, exclusively against real offenders—such as the defendant in *Williams*, who was peddling what he advertised as photos of men molesting his four-year-old daughter. Meanwhile, in the unlikely event an overzealous prosecutor were to stretch the law to criminalize, say, a news organization's good-faith video reporting on the abuse of children, that organization could still challenge the law "as applied" to itself.

It seems sensible to us not to throw the baby out with the bathwater. Since the Court doesn't always see it that way when the First Amendment is involved, we're relieved that the justices vindicated democratic choice, putting off what Justice Scalia aptly called "fanciful hypotheticals" until such a time as they may arise in real-world cases.

> "Even the Religious Right should be wary of a law that for the first time makes it possible to prosecute someone for what they merely think."

# The PROTECT Act Permits Prosecution of People for What They Think

*Frederick Lane*

*Frederick Lane is an author and lecturer who has written several books and has appeared on major television programs. In the following commentary on* United States v. Williams, *he explains the background of the PROTECT Act and argues that it is unconstitutional because it allows people to be prosecuted merely for what they think or believe. The law makes it illegal to advertise or present any material in such a way as to lead someone to believe it contains child pornography. Everyone agrees that child pornography is bad and that its distribution should be prevented, Lane says. However, under the PROTECT Act, someone could be prosecuted for offering material merely believed or alleged to contain pornography, even if it actually did not—for example, if it did not depict real children—and was therefore not illegal in itself. Thus for the first time a belief has become grounds for prosecution, and, in Lane's opinion, this is a violation of the First Amendment.*

Frederick Lane, "What Were They Thinking? *United States v. Williams* and Free Speech," *Beacon Broadside*, June 26, 2008. Copyright © 2008 Beacon Press. All rights reserved. Reproduced by permission of author.

The United States Supreme Court handed down [in May 2008] a decision in *United States v. Williams* that upheld the consitutionality of the Prosecutorial Remedies and Other Tools to end the Exploitation of Children Today Act of 2003 (The PROTECT Act). The 7-2 decision is the latest in a disturbing line of Congressional actions and Supreme Court decisions that cloak encroachments on the First Amendment in the pious garb of protecting children.

A little background is useful in understanding the implications of the *Williams* decision. It is fair to say that the United States is unparalleled among the nations of the world in its tolerance of speech. From the instant it is uttered, virtually all speech is presumed to be protected by the First Amendment. That presumption can be overcome, but only if a prosecutor or plaintiff can prove that the speech falls into one the recognized exceptions to the First Amendment: libel or slander, for instance, or obscenity.

There is only one category of speech that does not enjoy the presumption of First Amendment protection: child pornography, which has traditionally been defined as sexually explicit visual depictions of individuals under the age of 18. If a prosecutor can prove that the subject of a sexually explicit photograph, for instance, is under the age of 18 then, regardless of how artistic or socially significant the photo may be, it is still "obscene" and not protected by the First Amendment.

In response to a surge in the production and distribution of child pornography in the late 1970s and early 1980s, the federal and state governments passed laws making it a crime to possess child pornography. Although the Supreme Court has held that mere possession of obscenity is protected by the First Amendment (*Stanley v. Georgia* [1969]), it agreed that possession of child pornography could be barred (*New York v. Ferber* [1982]).

"The prevention of sexual exploitation and abuse of children," Justice Byron White wrote, "constitutes a government objective of surpassing importance." Among other things, he noted, the New York legislature found that child pornography serves as a "permanent record" of abuse, a harm that is perpetuated by continued circulation of the images. The legislature also declared (and the Court agreed) that penalizing consumers would lessen demand for child pornography and help to fight its production. Regardless of one's position on the political spectrum, there is virtually no disagreement that a ban on both the production and possession of actual child pornography is a good social policy.

The Court's ratification of a flat ban on child pornography had a relatively minimal impact on the First Amendment. Admittedly, the ruling did cause serious problems for some photographers, ranging from parents taking innocuous photos of their children to fine art photographers whose works included nude photos of children. . . . But on the whole, it was relatively easy to draw a bright line between legal and illegal images, and law enforcement made substantial progress in fighting child pornography.

## The Impact of New Technologies

Most of those gains, however, have been wiped out by computers, the Internet, and digital cameras, all of which have made the production and distribution of child pornography vastly easier and far more difficult to combat. These new technologies have also blurred the previously bright line between legal and illegal images: many websites feature very young-looking but still adult models; some individuals use software to blend two or more legal images into composite child pornography; and others use animation software to create completely artificial (but increasingly realistic) child pornography images.

In 1996, Congress adopted the Child Pornography Prevention Act as part of an omnibus appropriations bill. Among other things, the CPPA made it a crime to possess or distribute digital representations of minors engaged in sexual activity, even if the persons in the image were not actual minors. In *Ashcroft v. Free Speech Coalition* (2002), however, the Supreme Court ruled (by a 6-1-2 vote) that the CPPA was unconstitutional because it criminalized speech legitimately protected by the First Amendment.

"The CPPA," Justice [Anthony] Kennedy wrote, "prohibits speech despite its serious literary, artistic, political, or scientific value. The statute proscribes the visual depiction of an idea—that of teenagers engaging in sexual activity—that is a fact of modern society and has been a theme in art and literature throughout the ages."

The Court's decision was widely criticized by conservatives, and in particular, by the evangelical wing of the Republican Party, which has been at the forefront of Congressional efforts to restrict sexual materials online. It is no accident that in his recent speech on judicial activism, Senator John McCain alluded to the *Free Speech Coalition* decision as an example of activist judges.

In response to the *Free Speech Coalition* decision, Congress passed the PROTECT Act, which dropped the outright ban on "virtual" child pornography. Instead, the law makes it illegal to advertise or present any material in such a way as to lead someone to believe that the material contains "an obscene visual depiction of a minor engaging in sexually explicit conduct," or "a visual depiction of an actual minor engaging in sexually explicit conduct."

"Both the State and Federal Governments have sought to suppress it for many years," Justice Antonin Scalia wrote, "only to find it proliferating through the new medium of the Internet. This Court held unconstitutional Congress's previous attempt to meet this new threat, and Congress responded with a carefully crafted attempt to eliminate the First Amendment problems we identified. As far as the provision at issue in this case is concerned, that effort was successful."

## Prosecution for Mere Belief

The dissent in *Williams* was written by the Supreme Court justice the Religious Right most despises, David Souter. Along with Justice Ruth Bader Ginsburg, Souter argued that the PROTECT Act is constitutionally flawed because an individual could be prosecuted for advertising or selling an image that is not itself illegal (a sexually explicit photograph, for instance, that does not depict actual children), but which the buyer or seller simply believes is illegal.

"We should hold that a transaction in what turns out to be fake pornography is better understood," Justice Souter said, "not as an incomplete attempt to commit a crime, but as a completed series of intended acts that simply do not add up to a crime, owing to the privileged character of the material the parties were in fact about to deal in."

While recognizing the gravity of the problem being addressed by Congress, Souter suggested that the harm to the First Amendment is much more significant. Traditionally, he said, limitations on speech are grounded on "realistic, factual assessments of harm." Instead, the PROTECT Act bases its criminal prosecutions on "nothing more than a speaker's statement about the material itself, a statement that may disclose no more than his own belief about the subjects represented or his desire to foster belief in another."

"First Amendment freedoms," Justice Souter quoted from the *Free Speech Coalition* case, "are most in danger when the government seeks to control thought or to justify its laws for that impermissible end. The right to think is the beginning of freedom, and speech must be protected from the government because speech is the beginning of thought."

It is worth reiterating time and again that child pornography is a serious crime and a growing problem for law enforcement, and that all available resources should be devoted to preventing its production and prosecuting its distribution. But even the Religious Right should be wary of a law that for the first time makes it possible to prosecute someone for what they merely think.

CHAPTER 5

# Antispam Laws Applicable to Political E-mail Are Unconstitutional

# Case Overview

## *Jaynes v. Commonwealth of Virginia* (2008)

The increasing amount of spam is one of the Internet's most serious problems. According to a monthly spam report issued by Symantec Messaging and Web Security, over 79 percent of all e-mail sent in late January of 2009 was spam—and the percentage was even higher throughout most of 2008, before the shutdown of a host that many spammers used. This is a costly burden on the efficiency of the Internet, as well as a major inconvenience to anyone with an e-mail account. Nobody wants spam. It is not surprising, therefore, that laws have been passed attempting to limit it. None of these laws have had much effect, in part because over 75 percent of spam originates outside the United States. But they do help to deter the worst U.S. offenders.

Jeremy Jaynes, who was estimated to be one of the ten top spammers in the world, was the first person to be convicted of a felony solely for spamming—that is, without being accused of any associated crime such as fraud. From his home in North Carolina he had been sending out thousands of spam messages with forged headers every day. Although the messages originated in North Carolina, he was tried and convicted in Virginia because the messages were delivered by servers located in Virginia and he had known that they would be. He was sentenced to nine years in prison, but his incarceration was postponed pending appeal.

Virginia's antispam law, which was then new, made it a felony to send more than ten thousand unsolicited bulk e-mail messages with falsified headers in a twenty-four-hour period, one hundred thousand in a thirty-day period, or one million in a year. It might seem that there could be no objection to such a law other than by spammers. Jaynes's appeal that it was an unconstitutional law struck some observers as ridiculous; however, the law was not limited to felonies. Under it, sending lesser amounts of unsolicited bulk e-mail with falsified headers was defined as a misdemeanor. This, his attorney claimed, made it illegal to communicate anonymously, as there was no way for e-mail to remain completely anonymous unless its header was falsified. And the right to anonymous expression is protected under the First Amendment guarantee of free speech. To prohibit anonymous commercial mail would be permissible, but the law was not confined to commerical mail—it covered all mail, including political and religious mail, which cannot be restricted.

Both the Court of Appeals and the Virginia Supreme Court rejected this argument on the grounds that because Jaynes' e-mail was commercial, he did not have standing to use it. His attorney then petitioned the Virginia Supreme Court to reconsider the case. Though it is extremely rare for a court to do that, the request was granted. After reviewing it again, the Virginia Supreme Court ruled four to three that the antispam law was overbroad because it applied to more cases than it was meant to cover. If the anonymous political writings of America's founders were being published in Virginia today by e-mail, said the Court, they would be illegal. Therefore the law was unconstitutional, and Jaynes' conviction was overturned.

This ruling applies only to Virginia, and its attorney general appealed the decision to the U.S. Supreme Court, which refused review. An amicus curiae (friend of the court) brief filed by the Criminal Justice Legal Foundation points out that the antispam law does not prohibit anonymous e-mail because it is untrue that only false headers can make e-mail anonymous.

"[The Virginia antispam] statute is unconstitutionally overbroad on its face
because it prohibits ... speech protected
by the First Amendment to the United
States Constitution."

# The Court's Opinion:
# Virginia's Antispam Law
# Is Too Broad

### G. Steven Agee

At the time the following opinion was written, G. Steven Agee
was a justice of the Virginia Supreme Court. He has since become a judge on the U.S. Court of Appeals for the Fourth Circuit. In his opinion in Jaynes v. Virginia, Agee explains why the
court ruled that Virginia's law against spamming was unconstitutional. Although Jaynes sent spam from outside Virginia, the
state had jurisdiction over him because he knew that it would be
routed through mail servers located there. Virginia asserted that
its antispam law did not violate the Constitution's First Amendment—in other words, that it did not restrict freedom of
speech—because the servers were private property and to send
spam over them was the same as trespassing. However, Agee argues, the law prohibited not the unauthorized use of mail servers, but the use of false addresses on bulk mail. Using a false address is the only way to send e-mail anonymously, he contends,
and the right to speak anonymously is protected under the First
Amendment. There was nothing in the law that limited it to
fraudulent or unsolicited commercial mail; it could also be ap-

G. Steven Agee, opinion, *Jeremy Jaynes v. Commonwealth of Virginia*, Virginia Supreme
Court, September 12, 2008. Reproduced by permission.

*plied to anonymous religious or political mail. Therefore, it was too broad, and for that reason it violated the Constitution.*

From his home in Raleigh, North Carolina, [Jeremy] Jaynes used several computers, routers and servers to send over 10,000 e-mails within a 24-hour period to subscribers of America Online, Inc. (AOL) on each of three separate occasions. On July 16, 2003, Jaynes sent 12,197 pieces of unsolicited e-mail with falsified routing and transmission information onto AOL's proprietary network. On July 19, 2003, he sent 24,172, and on July 26, 2003, he sent 19,104. None of the recipients of the e-mails had requested any communication from Jaynes. He intentionally falsified the header information and sender domain names before transmitting the e-mails to the recipients. However, investigators used a sophisticated database search to identify Jaynes as the sender of the e-mails. Jaynes was arrested and charged with violating [the Virginia antispam law], which provides in relevant part:

A. Any person who:

1. Uses a computer or computer network with the intent to falsify or forge electronic mail transmission information or other routing information in any manner in connection with the transmission of unsolicited bulk electronic mail [UBE] through or into the computer network of an electronic mail service provider or its subscribers ... is guilty of a Class 1 misdemeanor.

B. A person is guilty of a Class 6 felony if he commits a violation of subsection A and:

1. The volume of UBE transmitted exceeded 10,000 attempted recipients in any 24-hour period, 100,000 attempted recipients in any 30-day time period, or one million attempted recipients in any one-year time period. . . .

While executing a search of Jaynes' home, police discovered a cache of compact discs (CDs) containing over 176 million full e-mail addresses and 1.3 billion e-mail user names. The search also led to the confiscation of storage discs which contained AOL e-mail address information and other personal and private account information for millions of AOL subscribers. The AOL user information had been stolen from AOL by a former employee and was in Jaynes' possession. . . .

Jaynes moved to dismiss the charges against him on the grounds that the statute violated the dormant Commerce Clause, was unconstitutionally vague, and violated the First Amendment. The circuit court denied that motion. . . .

A jury convicted Jaynes of three counts of violating [the law], and the circuit court sentenced Jaynes to three years in prison on each count, with the sentences to run consecutively for an active term of imprisonment of nine years. The [Virginia] Court of Appeals affirmed his convictions. We awarded Jaynes an appeal.

## Virginia Had Jurisdiction over Jaynes

Jaynes makes four assignments of error to the judgment of the Court of Appeals. First, he assigns error to the determination that the circuit court had jurisdiction over him on the crimes charged. Second, Jaynes contends [that the law] "abridge[s] the First Amendment right to anonymous speech," and it was error not to reverse his convictions on that basis. Separately, Jaynes assigns as error the failure of the Court of Appeals to hold that [the law] is void for vagueness. Lastly, Jaynes posits that the statute violates the Commerce Clause of the United States Constitution.

Jaynes asserts that the Court of Appeals erred in holding that the circuit court had jurisdiction over him for violating [the law] because he did not "use" a computer in Virginia. He contends that a violation of that statute can occur only in the location where the e-mail routing information is falsified. Jaynes maintains that because he only used computers to send the e-mails from his home in Raleigh, North Carolina, he committed no crime in Virginia. Further, because he had no control over the routing of the e-mails, he argues his actions did not have an "immediate result" in Virginia, and under *Moreno v. Baskerville*, could not be the basis for jurisdiction over him by Virginia courts. Therefore, according to Jaynes, the circuit court had no jurisdiction over him and his convictions are void....

Jaynes argues that he "merely sent e-mails that happened to be routed through AOL servers." We disagree. As the evidence established, all e-mail must flow through the recipient's e-mail server in order to reach the intended recipient. By selecting AOL subscribers as his e-mail recipients, Jaynes knew and intended that his e-mails would utilize AOL servers because he clearly intended to send to users whose e-mails ended in "@aol.com." The evidence established that the AOL servers are located in Virginia, and that the location of AOL's servers was information easily accessible to the general public. Applying our standard of review to the evidence presented along with all reasonable inferences therefrom, we conclude that the evidence supports the conclusion that Jaynes knew and intended that the e-mails he sent to AOL subscribers would utilize AOL's servers which are located in Virginia. Thus an intended and necessary result of Jaynes' action, the e-mail transmission through the computer network, occurred in Virginia.

Furthermore, a state may exercise jurisdiction over criminal acts that are committed outside the state, but are intended to, and do in fact, produce harm within the state....

## Restricting First Amendment Rights

Jaynes next contends that [the Virginia antispam law] is constitutionally deficient as overbroad under the First Amendment and therefore the statute cannot be enforced. He argues the Court of Appeals erred in affirming the circuit court's ruling denying his motion to dismiss on that basis....

Jaynes does not make a pure facial challenge to [the antispam law] as he does not argue "that no set of circumstances exists under which the Act would be valid." *United States v. Salerno*. Similarly, Jaynes does not make an "as-applied challenge" to the statute, meaning he does not contend the application of the statute to the actual acts for which he was convicted violates the First Amendment. Instead, Jaynes challenges the statute by claiming it is unconstitutional as overbroad. That is, Jaynes contends that because the statute could potentially reach the protected speech of a third party, he (Jaynes) is entitled to claim exoneration for his otherwise unprotected speech.

The Commonwealth contends Jaynes has no standing to raise a First Amendment overbreadth defense. . . .

In 1925, the United States Supreme Court enunciated the principle "that freedom of speech and of the press—which are protected by the First Amendment from abridgement by Congress—are among the fundamental personal rights and 'liberties' protected by the due process clause of the Fourteenth Amendment from impairment by the States." *Gitlow v. New York.* . . .

To accept the Commonwealth's view . . . would permit, under the guise of standing, a state court to ignore the substantive constitutional rights of citizens in contravention of the Fourteenth Amendment. That is an untenable position because the right to assert the protection of the First Amendment (by overbreadth or otherwise) can no more be restricted by a state rule of standing than the exclusionary rule applied to impermissible searches and seizures could be limited by state evidence law. . . .

Accordingly, we hold Jaynes has standing to raise the First Amendment overbreadth claim.

## Antispam Law Is Not a Trespass Law

The Commonwealth argues, in the alternative, that if Jaynes has standing to raise a First Amendment overbreadth claim, that claim is not proper for consideration because his conduct was a form of trespass and thus not entitled to First Amendment protection. [The antispam law] in the Commonwealth's view, is like a trespass statute, prohibiting trespassing on the privately owned e-mail servers through the intentional use of false information and that no First Amendment protection is afforded in that circumstance. The Court of Appeals adopted this position and held Jaynes' First Amendment argument was "not relevant." *Jaynes v. Commonwealth*. Concluding that [the law] "prohibits lying to commit a trespass," the Court of Appeals determined the "statute proscribes intentional falsity as a machination to make massive, uncompensated use of the private property of an ISP [Internet service provider]. Therefore, the statute cannot be overbroad because no protected speech whatsoever falls within its purview." We disagree.

Trespass is the unauthorized use of or entry onto another's property.

Significantly, [the law] does not prohibit the *unauthorized* use of privately owned e-mail servers. The statute only prohibits the intentional use of false routing information in connection with sending certain e-mail through such servers. Thus, even if an e-mail service provider specifically allowed persons using false IP [Internet protocol] addresses and domain names to use its server, the sender could be prosecuted under [the antispam law] although there was no unauthorized use or trespass. Therefore, [the law] is not a trespass statute.

The Commonwealth's argument that there is no First Amendment right to use false identification to gain access to private property is inapposite [irrelevant]. First, in making this argument the Commonwealth uses the terms "false" and "fraudulent" interchangeably. Those concepts are not synonymous. At issue here is the statute's prohibition of "false" routing information. Second, the cases upon which the Commonwealth relies are civil cases between Internet service providers and the entities engaged in sending commercial unsolicited bulk e-mails. In litigation between these private parties, the courts have held that the unauthorized use of the Internet service providers' property constituted common law trespass and that a First Amendment claim could not be raised against the owner of private property. These cases have no relevance here because this is not a trespass action by a private property owner and the First Amendment right is not being asserted against the owner of private property, but against government action impacting the claimed First Amendment right. Accordingly, we reject the Commonwealth's argument and hold the Court of Appeals erred in this regard.

## Constitutional Right to Anonymous Speech

We now turn to Jaynes' contention that [the Virginia antispam law] is unconstitutionally overbroad. To address this challenge, we first review certain technical aspects of the transmission of e-mails. In transmitting and receiving e-mails, the e-mail servers use a protocol which prescribes what information one computer must send to another. This SMTP [simple mail transfer protocol] requires that the routing information contain an IP address and a domain name for the sender and recipient of each e-mail. Domain names and IP addresses are assigned to Internet servers by private organizations through a registration process. To obtain an IP address or domain name, the registrant pays a fee and provides identifying contact information to the registering organization. The domain names and IP addresses are contained in a searchable database which can associate the domain name with an IP address and vice versa.

The IP address and domain name do not directly identify the sender, but if the IP address or domain name is acquired from a registering organization, a database search of the address or domain name can eventually lead to the contact information on file with the registration organizations. A sender's IP address or domain name which is not registered will not prevent the transmission of the e-mail; however, the identity of the sender may not be discoverable through a database search and use of registration contact information.

As shown by the record, because e-mail transmission protocol requires entry of an IP address and domain name for the sender, the only way such a speaker can publish an anonymous e-mail is to enter a false IP address or domain name. Therefore, . . . registered IP addresses and domain names discoverable through searchable data bases and registration documents "necessarily result[] in a surrender of [the speaker's] anonymity." *Watchtower Bible & Tract Society v. Village of Stratton.* The right to engage in anonymous speech, particularly anonymous political or religious speech, is "an aspect of the freedom of speech protected by the First Amendment." *McIntyre v. Ohio Elections Comm'n.* By prohibiting false routing information in the dissemination of e-mails, [the law] infringes on that protected right. The Supreme Court has characterized regulations prohibiting such anonymous speech as "a direct regulation of the content of speech."

State statutes that burden "core political speech," as this statute does, are presumptively invalid and subject to a strict scrutiny test. Under that test a statute will be deemed constitutional only if it is narrowly drawn to further a compelling state interest. . . .

There is no dispute that [the antispam law] was enacted to control the transmission of unsolicited commercial bulk e-mail, generally referred to as spam. In enacting the federal CAN-SPAM Act, Congress stated that commercial bulk e-mail threatened the efficiency and convenience of e-mail. Many other states have regulated unsolicited bulk e-mail but, unlike Virginia, have restricted such regulation to commercial e-mails. There is nothing in the record or arguments of the parties, however, suggesting that unsolicited non-commercial bulk e-mails were the target of this legislation, caused increased costs to the Internet service providers, or were otherwise a focus of the problem sought to be addressed by the General Assembly through its enactment of [the law].

Jaynes does not contest the Commonwealth's interest in controlling unsolicited commercial bulk e-mail as well as fraudulent or otherwise illegal e-mail. Nevertheless, [the law] is not limited to instances of commercial or fraudulent transmission of e-mail, nor is it restricted to transmission of illegal or otherwise unprotected speech such as pornography or defamation speech. Therefore, viewed under the strict scrutiny standard, [the law] is not narrowly tailored to protect the compelling interests advanced by the Commonwealth.

## Law Is Substantially Overbroad

The Commonwealth argues that we should not preclude enforcement of [the antispam law] because, even if unconstitutionally overbroad, that remedy is limited to those statutes that are substantially overbroad. . . . Recognizing the sweep of this remedy, the United States Supreme Court has stated that it will not impose such an expansive result where the chilling effect of an overbroad statute on constitutionally protected rights cannot justify prohibiting all enforcement of the law. . . . Thus a statute should be declared facially overbroad and unconstitutional only if the statute "punishes a 'substantial' amount of protected free speech, 'judged in relation to the statute's plainly legitimate sweep.'" *Virginia v. Hicks.*

The Commonwealth argues that [the law] is not substantially overbroad because it does not impose any restrictions on the content of the e-mail and "most" applications of its provisions would be constitutional, citing its application to unsolicited bulk commercial e-mail, unsolicited bulk e-mail that proposes a criminal transaction, and unsolicited bulk e-mail that is defamatory or contains obscene images. According to the Commonwealth an "imagine[d] hypothetical situation where the Act might be unconstitutional as applied does not render the Act substantially overbroad."

The United States Supreme Court recently reviewed the First Amendment overbreadth doctrine in *United States v. Williams.* The Court noted

> [i]n order to maintain an appropriate balance, we have vigorously enforced the requirement that a statute's overbreadth be substantial, not only in an absolute sense, but also relative to the statute's plainly legitimate sweep.
>
> . . . [I]t is impossible to determine whether a statute reaches too far without first knowing what the statute covers.

Applying that inquiry under *Williams* in this case is relatively straightforward as [the antispam law] would prohibit all bulk e-mail containing anonymous political, religious, or other expressive speech. For example, were the *Federalist Papers* just being published today via e-mail, that transmission by Publius [the name used by the authors] would violate the statute. Such an expansive scope of unconstitutional coverage is not what the Court in *Williams* referenced "as the tendency of our overbreadth doctrine to summon forth an endless stream of fanciful hypotheticals." We thus reject the Commonwealth's argument that Jaynes' facial challenge to [the law] must fail because the statute is not "substantially overbroad."

Lastly, the Commonwealth asserts that we need not declare [the law] unconstitutional because a limiting construction can be adopted by this Court that would prevent invalidating the statute. Such a construction according to the Commonwealth would be a declaration that the statute does not apply to "unsolicited bulk non-commercial e-mail that does not involve criminal activity, defamation or obscene materials." Alternatively the Commonwealth suggests that we hold the statute applies only in instances where the receiving Internet service provider "actually objects to the bulk e-mail." . . .

The construction urged by the Commonwealth is not a reasonable construction of the statute. Nothing in the statute suggests the limited applications advanced by the Commonwealth. If we adopted the Commonwealth's suggested construction we would be rewriting [the law] in a material and substantive way. Such a task lies within the province of the General Assembly, not the courts.

For the foregoing reasons, we hold that the circuit court properly had jurisdiction over Jaynes. We also hold that Jaynes has standing to raise a First Amendment overbreadth claim as to [the Virginia antispam law]. That statute is unconstitutionally overbroad on its face because it prohibits the anonymous transmission of all unsolicited bulk e-mails including those containing political, religious or other speech protected by the First Amendment to the United States Constitution. Accordingly, we will reverse the judgment of the Court of Appeals and vacate Jaynes' convictions.

*"Anti-spam organizations and law enforcement officials see prosecutions as key in the fight, along with software development and consumer education."*

# Enforcing Antispam Laws Is Key in the Fight Against Spam

*Emma Schwartz*

*At the time this article was written, Emma Schwartz was a staff writer for the* Los Angeles Times. *In the following article she reports that Jeremy Jaynes, one of the top ten spammers in the world, was convicted under a new Virginia state law against sending fraudulent unsolicited e-mail messages. The jury recommended that he be sentenced to nine years in prison. Antispam advocates hope that the case and others that are pending will send a message to spammers through the world, Schwartz says. They see prosecutions as a key tactic in reducing the amount of spam. Although some states are beginning to catch spammers through regular fraud laws, officials believe that specific laws making spam a felony have greater deterrent effect. However, they caution that such laws will be effective only if they are persistently enforced, and it is uncertain whether federal and state authorities will enforce them.*

From a nondescript house in a neighboring state, Jeremy Jaynes and his sister raked in more than $24 million from fake Internet offers of penny-stock picker schemes, nonexistent FedEx refunds, cheap drugs and pornography.

They did it by flooding the inboxes of millions of Internet users with junk e-mails known as spam. Indeed, Jaynes was ranked among the top 10 spammers in the world.

But . . . Jaynes' schemes fell victim to what government officials and anti-spam groups hope will become an increasingly effective weapon against Internet fraud: hefty doses of time behind bars.

Using a new state anti-spam law that is considered the toughest in the nation, a Virginia jury convicted North Carolina residents Jaynes and Jessica DeGroot of sending untraceable junk e-mails to millions of customers of America Online, which is based in Dulles, Va.

It was the first conviction under the law, the first in the nation to make it a felony to send large numbers of fraudulent, unsolicited e-mail messages.

In a state that is home to some of the nations' largest Internet service providers, the jury's decision was a milestone in another way: It made it likely that Jaynes would serve substantial prison time. The . . . jury recommended nine years.

DeGroot, 28, who was found to have played only a supporting role in her brother's activities, was fined $7,500. A third defendant was acquitted. Jaynes' lawyer is contesting the prosecutions.

Although building legal cases against spammers and bringing them to court can be difficult given the global nature of the Internet, state officials and anti-spam advocates hoped this case and others in the works would reverberate beyond the mid-Atlantic region—much the way high-profile legal action has put a crimp in the illegal downloading of music from the Internet.

"These convictions and the prison sentence for kingpin spammer Jaynes send a resounding message from Virginia to spammers around the world," said Richard Campbell, deputy attorney general for the commonwealth. "If you defraud individuals and encumber ISPs with illegal spam, there are consequences."

Spam has confounded government and private sector officials for years. Despite hundreds of civil lawsuits, and a bundle of federal and state laws, the unsolicited e-mails now account for 70% of all e-mail traffic, according to anti-spam organizations.

It's a lucrative business for spammers. Jaynes was accused of forging Internet addresses and using confidential e-mail directories stolen from Internet providers like AOL to peddle his usually phony products. In one month alone, he received 10,000 credit card orders for $39.95 each, according to prosecutors.

Anti-spam organizations and law enforcement officials see prosecutions as key in the fight, along with software development and consumer education.

As a high-tech hub that sees nearly three-fourths of Internet traffic flow through its borders, Virginia is poised to take on more cases.

"Virginia has the potential of setting the pace of how to set penalties that may actually have an effect in dissuading the behavior," said Ray Everett-Church, who works with the anti-spam group Coalition Against Unsolicited Commercial Email. "But the reality is there is no one solution to spam, and it's going to require a mixture of techniques and approaches to really bring some change to the environment."

Some states are beginning to nab spammers through regular fraud or identity-theft statues. Officials seized $50 million in assets from Arizona spammers [in 2003]. And in May in New York, "Buffalo Spammer" Howard Carmack was convicted and sentenced to as many as seven years in prison.

Now other states, including Michigan and Maryland, have made unsolicited spam a felony. Though these states could use older statutes, officials say having a specific spam law makes prosecution easier and sends a clearer message.

Criminal prosecution is also making its way to the federal level. A new federal statute, which took effect in January [2004], was modeled after Virginia's law. It makes it illegal to send unsolicited bulk e-mails that are not accurately labeled and do not have real return addresses.

In September, federal officials in California obtained the first conviction under the new Can Spam Act, prosecuting 28-year-old Nicholas Tombros, who drove around a Venice Beach community with a laptop computer looking for unprotected wireless Internet access points from which to send spam.

Federal officials said a number of other cases are pending.

But anti-spam advocates cautioned that prosecutions would have a deterrent effect only if enforcement was broad and persistent.

And it's unclear whether federal and state authorities will continue to step up enforcement. State budgets are thin. Tracking down spammers is tedious. And spammers continue to frustrate authorities with bolder methods such as sending spam through unsuspecting private computer users.

> *"I find it* extremely *difficult to imagine a circumstance in which [Virginia's antispam] restrictions would impinge on legitimate exercises of free speech."*

# Virginia's Antispam Law Would Not Ban Constitutionally Protected Speech

*Tim Lee*

*Tim Lee is an adjunct scholar at the Cato Institute, a Washington, D.C., libertarian think-tank, as well as a PhD student and member of the Center for Information Technology Policy at Princeton University. In the following viewpoint he argues that although he usually opposes attempts to restrict free speech, he does not think that the right to speak anonymously can be extended so far as to strike down Virginia's antispam law. To violate this law, he says, a spammer has to send more than ten thousand pieces of unsolicited e-mail with falsified headers in a single day. Lee argues that it is very hard to imagine a legitimate e-mail user doing this. In his opinion analogies to eighteenth-century pamphleteers are misleading because in the pre-Internet age there was no way to send tens of thousands of messages per day. Furthermore, he says, there is no "slippery slope" involved in this particular law because legitimate users who wish to remain anonymous have no reason to send that many messages. Therefore, he believes that the law does not violate the First Amendment.*

Tim Lee, "Anti-Spam Laws and the First Amendment," *Technology Liberation Front*, August 7, 2008. Reproduced by permission of the author.

I'm reading about the first-ever felony conviction for spamming [i.e., *Jaynes v. Commonwealth of Virginia*]. While I almost always agree with the ACLU [American Civil Liberties Union] on free speech issues, I found the Virginia ACLU's *amicus* [friend of the court] brief in the case totally unpersuasive.

The ACLU argues that the First Amendment protects a right to anonymous speech, which I wholeheartedly agree with. However, I don't think that right can be stretched so far as to strike down the Virginia anti-spam statute at issue in this case. This statute prohibited the falsification of email headers while sending more than 10,000 pieces of unsolicited bulk email. So this means that under the statute, someone may (a) send out an unlimited number of emails using a real email address, (b) send out 9999 emails per day (99,999 per month, 999,999 per year) while falsifying email headers, or (c) send out an unlimited number of emails with falsified addresses to people who have previously consented to receive them. I find it *extremely* difficult to imagine a circumstance in which these restrictions would impinge on legitimate exercises of free speech. The activities prohibited by this statute simply don't include the kinds of situations that motivate the constitutional protection of anonymous speech—defending a point of view or releasing sensitive information without fear of reprisal or public embarrassment. Whistleblowers might want to send falsified emails to a few dozen journalists, legislators, or business leaders, but I'm having trouble thinking of a plausible situation in which a whistle-blower had a genuine need to reach more than 10,000 people.

I find analogies to older technologies—and to 18th-century pamphleteers in particular—unpersuasive in this case because this case just isn't like anything that existed in the pre-Internet age. In 1975, there just wasn't any way to transmit tens of thousands of messages for a fraction of a penny per message. The costliness of information transmission—any available communications technology cost at least a few pennies per message—meant that the law never had to grapple with the possibility that sending messages could become a significant enough nuisance to require regulation. Now we *do* live in that world, and I think it's a mistake to put too much weight on misleading analogies to older communications technologies with vastly different properties.

## No Effect on Legitimate E-mail Users

A final reason anti-spam legislation doesn't bother me from a First Amendment perspective is that I don't see any slippery slope here. Not only is the activity being targeted unambiguously bad, but there are very few grey areas, and the grey areas are pretty bad themselves. The Virginia statute applies two very clear bright lines—spam must be unsolicited and it must consist of more than 10,000 pieces in a 24-hour period—that make it trivially easy for anyone interested in following the law to do so. Moreover, thanks to the growth of spam filters, there is an enormous gulf between bad spammers and legitimate email users. Legitimate users who did vaguely spam-like things (say, a non-profit organization that sent out a fundraising appeal to people who hadn't consented to receive it) would get most of their spam blocked by ISPs' [Internet service providers'] spam filters and would get contacted by email administrators very promptly to be told to knock it off. It's hard to imagine such an organization breaking Virginia's law (sending out 10,000 copies and forging email headers), and even if it did it's hard to imagine a prosecutor going after them. Which means that only spammers are engaging in spammer-like behavior. It's pretty easy to write a statute that criminalizes most spammers and few if any legitimate email users. To use the Supreme Court's lingo, Virginia's spam law strikes me as "narrowly tailored" to blocking an undisputed evil and is no more restrictive than is necessary to accomplish that objective. If there's any speech restriction that should pass First Amendment scrutiny, this is it.

None of this is to say that some anti-spam laws can't be too broad. [The federal antispam law] CAN-SPAM, for example, appears to criminalize the sending of "multiple" deceptive emails or the creation of more than five separate email accounts for sending commercial emails. I can certainly think of grey areas for *those* kinds of prohibitions, and would have serious doubts about their constitutionality.

*"If James Madison, Alexander Hamilton and John Jay were alive and publishing under the false name 'Publius' today, they would be prime candidates for prosecution under Virginia's anti-spam law."*

# Under Antispam Laws America's Founding Fathers Would Be Criminals

*John W. Whitehead*

*John W. Whitehead is a constitutional attorney and author. He is the founder and president of the Rutherford Institute, a civil liberties organization. In the following viewpoint he argues that Virginia's antispam law is a threat to average citizens because even though a spammer must send out more than ten thousand anonymous unsolicited e-mails in one day to be charged with a felony, someone who sends fewer than that can be charged with a misdemeanor. The right to free speech includes the right to speak anonymously, he says. America's founding fathers—such as James Madison and Alexander Hamilton—published their political views under false names, and if they were alive today they would probably use the Internet to do so, yet Virginia's law would make them criminals, argues Whitehead. In Whitehead's opinion, the Virginia Supreme Court was right to rule that the state's antispam law violates the First Amendment.*

John W. Whitehead, "Under Anti-Spam Laws, the Founding Fathers Would Be Criminals Today," *Rutherford Institute*, September 22, 2008. Copyright © 2008, The Rutherford Institute. Reproduced by permission.

The Internet, one of the great wonders of modern technology, has become the primary source of news and information for many people. Even more important, it may be the only place where many citizens have the opportunity to speak their minds and exercise their First Amendment rights. However, in recent years, federal and state governments have been attempting to gain control of the Internet and censor it. One of the more disturbing developments involves a law in Virginia.

Under Virginia's five-year-old [as of 2008] anti-spam law, anyone who sends out high volumes of spam email—either 10,000 messages within a 24-hour period or 100,000 in a 30-day period—and uses a fictitious name could be arrested and charged with a criminal felony.

The anti-spam law was used to prosecute Jeremy Jaynes, a prolific spammer from North Carolina. Convicted of using a false identity to send junk email and advertise penny stocks or a new career as a FedEx refund processor, Jaynes was sentenced to nine years in jail.

If Jaynes is in fact guilty of bilking people out of their hard-earned money, then he should be punished. But he wasn't prosecuted for perpetrating fraud on unsuspecting Americans. Instead, Jaynes was targeted for sending out mass amounts of unsolicited email under an assumed name.

## A Threat to the Average Citizen

This is where the threat to the average citizen comes in. And it's where this spam legislation, which could have done some good in eliminating Internet scams, runs afoul of the First Amendment.

According to the anti-spam law, individuals who send out unsolicited bulk emails without providing their true identity could face misdemeanor charges, including up to twelve months in jail and a $2500 fine. But since the law does not define what "bulk" email is, presumably two or three emails would qualify.

For instance, let's say your next-door neighbor sends out an email to members of your community expressing his concerns about a local zoning ordinance. Fearing retaliation from local government officials, he decides to send the email under the pseudonym "John Doe." This simple act of exercising his right to freely speak and criticize the government under an assumed name is enough to get him fined and thrown in jail.

Finally, after years of wrangling in the courts, the Virginia Supreme Court recently held that the anti-spam law violates Jaynes' right to engage in anonymous speech. According to the court, this "is an aspect of the freedom of speech protected by the First Amendment." Although this is an important ruling, the Virginia Attorney General, who has vigorously pursued Jaynes, will most likely appeal the decision to the U.S. Supreme Court.

The U.S. Supreme Court, however, has recognized the importance of ensuring that average citizens have the right to use false names and publish anonymously. In its 1960 decision in *Talley v. California*, the Supreme Court ruled that a law forbidding individuals from distributing handbills without identifying their identity unconstitutionally infringed on the First Amendment's guarantee to free speech. The Court declared:

> Anonymous pamphlets, leaflets, brochures and even books have played an important role in the progress of mankind. Persecuted groups and sects from time to time throughout history have been able to criticize oppressive practices and laws either anonymously or not at all. . . . Before the Revolutionary War colonial patriots frequently had to conceal their authorship or distribution of literature that easily could have brought down on them prosecutions by English-controlled courts. . . . It is plain that anonymity has sometimes been assumed for the most constructive purposes.

## Today's Public Square

Many of America's founding fathers used false names when publishing their ideas about the future of American democracy. In fact, James Madison, Alexander Hamilton and John Jay used the name "Publius" when writing the Federalist Papers, a series of articles in support of the ratification of the recently drafted Constitution.

The right to free speech includes the right to speak with anonymity. And nowhere is free speech exercised more prolifically than on the worldwide web. The Internet has become a critical forum for individuals to freely share information and express their ideas. Like the historical public square, which has slowly been crowded out by shopping malls and parking lots, the Internet is an open forum that provides its users with a worldwide stage. It not only allows "John Doe" to express his disfavor with a local zoning ordinance, it also allows people all over the nation and the world to have a voice.

Of course, spam is a nuisance and an inconvenience. No one likes junk email. Yet nowhere in the U.S. Constitution does it say that we have a right to be free from annoying speech.

Consider this: If James Madison, Alexander Hamilton and John Jay were alive and publishing under the false name "Publius" today, they would be prime candidates for prosecution under Virginia's anti-spam law. And they would most likely be using the Internet to get their message out to as many fellow citizens as possible. As a result, they could very well be arrested for speaking their minds on important issues of the day. Had that happened, Jay might never have become the first Chief Justice of the U.S. Supreme Court. Hamilton might never have been a major force in setting economic policy for the U.S. and Madison, considered the Father of the Constitution, might never have written the First Amendment, which to this day guarantees our right to free speech.

*"Virginia Attorney General Robert F. McDonnell (R) promptly said he would appeal the case to the U.S. Supreme Court."*

# The Ruling on Virginia's Antispam Law Will Be Appealed to the U.S. Supreme Court

*Tom Jackman*

*Tom Jackman is a staff writer for* The Washington Post. *In the following article he describes the reactions to the ruling in* Jaynes v. Virgina, *which Virginia's attorney general plans to appeal to the U.S. Supreme Court. The state supreme court had decided that Virginia's antispam law was unconstitutional because it was not restricted to commercial or fraudulent spam, but might also cover types of speech that are protected by the First Amendment. The law prohibited the use of false addresses in bulk e-mail, yet the right to speak anonymously is part of the right to free speech, and for that reason it was struck down. Internet service providers, however, said that no one has the right to use their privately owned servers deceptively for the purpose of sending unsolicited e-mail, regardless of its content.*

The Virginia Supreme Court yesterday [September 12, 2008,] ruled that the state's anti-spam law, designed to prevent the sending of masses of unwanted e-mail, violates the First Amendment right to freedom of speech.

Virginia Attorney General Robert F. McDonnell (R) promptly said he would appeal the case to the U.S. Supreme Court. The law was one of the first enacted in the United States to stem the overwhelming tide of unwanted e-mail. The 2004 trial in Loudoun County of mass e-mailer Jeremy Jaynes resulted in the first felony conviction in the country for spamming.

But the state Supreme Court said the law doesn't make any distinction between types of e-mail or types of speech, and so it was unconstitutional. The ruling came on an appeal of Jaynes's conviction. Jaynes had sent the mass e-mails anonymously by using false Internet addresses, and the court said that speech is also protected by the First Amendment.

Justice G. Steven Agee, who has since moved to the U.S. Court of Appeals for the 4th Circuit, wrote the unanimous opinion for the court. "The right to engage in anonymous speech, particularly anonymous political or religious speech, is 'an aspect of the freedom of speech protected by the First Amendment,'" Agee wrote, citing a 1995 U.S. Supreme Court case. "By prohibiting false routing information in the dissemination of e-mails," the court ruled, Virginia's anti-spam law "infringes on that protected right."

Agee noted that "were the 'Federalist Papers' just being published today via e-mail, that transmission by 'Publius' would violate the [Virginia] statute." Publius was the pen name for James Madison, Alexander Hamilton and John Jay.

## Not Limited to Commercial Spam

The court determined that the law does not limit its restrictions on spam to commercial or fraudulent e-mail or to such unprotected speech as obscenity or defamation. Many other states and the federal government drafted anti-spam laws after Virginia, but often specifically restricted the regulations to commercial e-mails, the court found. The ruling affects only the Virginia statute.

McDonnell called the law an innovative act that broke new ground in protecting citizens, and he noted that Jaynes was rated one of the most prolific spammers in the world. Loudoun Circuit Court Judge Thomas D. Horne sentenced Jaynes, of Raleigh, N.C., to nine years in prison but allowed Jaynes to remain free while his appeals were heard.

"The Supreme Court of Virginia," McDonnell said in a statement, "has erroneously ruled that one has a right to deceptively enter somebody else's private property for purposes of distributing his unsolicited fraudulent e-mails.... We will take this issue directly to the Supreme Court of the United States. The right of citizens to be free from unwanted fraudulent e-mails is one that I believe must be made secure."

The court's ruling was remarkable for another reason: It reversed its own ruling of six months ago, when the court upheld the anti-spam law by a 4 to 3 margin. But Jaynes's attorneys asked the court to reconsider, typically a long shot in appellate law, and the court not only reconsidered but changed its mind. Agee wrote both opinions.

"I think the decision is a sound one," said Rodney A. Smolla, dean of the Washington and Lee University Law School and a First Amendment scholar. "This is a case in which the spammer may have been doing things that a well-crafted law could make illegal. The problem with the Virginia law is it included e-mail communications that people have the right to make anonymously."

There was plenty of disagreement, particularly among those who provide Internet service or battle spam.

"Horrendous," said Jon Praed of the Internet Law Group, which has represented America Online, Verizon and other Internet providers. "The idea that someone can intrude on someone else's mail server, because they might be reciting the Gettysburg Address? I guess a burglar can break into your home as long as they are reciting the Gettysburg Address."

Praed noted that spam is not likely to increase in Virginia just because the law has been struck; federal law also prohibits spam, spam filters screen much of it and expert spammers often are out of the country. But spam does provide links to dangerous and illegal places on the Web, particularly for young users, as well as inject viruses and other bad software into computers, giving lawmakers a compelling reason to regulate it, Praed said.

## 90 Percent of E-mail Is Spam

The U.S. Internet Service Providers Association estimated that 90 percent of e-mail is spam. Internet service providers "should not be required to bear the cost of the abuse of their e-mail networks," said Kate Dean, executive director of the association, which filed briefs in support of the law.

Jaynes was convicted by a jury of sending tens of thousands of e-mails through America Online servers in Loudoun. Jaynes's e-mails were advertising products to help pick stocks, erase one's Internet search history and obtain refunds from FedEx and contained hyperlinks within the e-mail redirecting the recipient to those businesses. His attorney Thomas M. Wolf of Richmond noted that there was nothing fraudulent about the e-mails; Jaynes was prosecuted simply for sending them en masse.

"Everybody hates spam," Wolf said. "The point is, you don't have to trample the Constitution to regulate spam."

Virginia's anti-spam law made it a misdemeanor to send unsolicited bulk e-mail by using false transmission information, such as a phony domain name or Internet Protocol address. The domain name is the name of the Internet host or account, such as "aol.com." The Internet Protocol is a series of numbers, separated by periods, assigned to specific computers. The crime becomes a felony if more than 10,000 recipients are mailed in a 24-hour period.

Chris Thompson, a spokesman for Spamhaus, an international nonprofit group that tracks and combats spammers, pointed out that unlicensed radio stations may not broadcast, only the Postal Service can place mail in mailboxes and loud sound[ing] trucks may not troll neighborhoods with impunity.

"None of those minor restrictions appear to infringe on a citizen's ability to express themselves freely," Thompson said. "Why the court would deny basic protections for ISP servers and bandwidth escapes us."

[Editor's note: The U.S Supreme Court refused to review the case, so the ruling stands.]

# Organizations to Contact

*The editors have compiled the following list of organizations concerned with the issues debated in this book. The descriptions are derived from materials provided by the organizations. All have publications or information available for interested readers. The list was compiled on the date of publication of the present volume; the information provided here may change. Be aware that many organizations take several weeks or longer to respond to inquiries, so allow as much time as possible.*

**Association of Telehealth Service Providers (ATSP)**
4702 SW Scholls Ferry Road #400
Portland, OR  97225-2008
(503) 922-0988 • fax: (315) 222-2402
e-mail: admin@atsp.org
Web site: www.atsp.org

The Association of Telehealth Service Providers is an international membership-based organization dedicated to improving health care through growth of the telehealth industry. Its Web site contains detailed information about the legal use of the Internet in the practice of medicine.

**Computer Crime Research Center (CCRC)**
Box 8010, Zaporozhye 95   69095
   Ukraine
Web site: www.crime-research.org

The Computer Crime Research Center is a nonprofit, nongovernmental scientific research organization that conducts research in legal, criminal, and criminological problems of cybercrime. Although it is based in Ukraine, its English site contains many articles about cybercrime from American and British sources as well as news and links.

## Criminal Justice Legal Foundation (CJLF)
PO Box 1199, Sacramento, California  95812
(916) 446-0345
Web site: www.cjlf.org

The Criminal Justice Legal Foundation is a public interest organization working to ensure that courts respect the rights of crime victims and law-abiding society. Its Web site contains an important amicus curiae (friend of the court) brief submitted to the U.S. Supreme Court in the case of *Jaynes v. Virginia.*

## Cybercrime Law
Web site: www.cybercrimelaw.net

Cybercrime Law is a global information clearinghouse on cybercrime law containing a comprehensive survey of current legislation from around the world that includes the laws of seventy-eight countries, plus news about cybercrime from around the world.

## Electronic Frontier Foundation (EFF)
454 Shotwell Street, San Francisco, CA  94110-1914
(415) 436-9333 • fax: (415) 436-9993
Web site: www.eff.org

The Electronic Frontier Foundation is the leading civil liberties group defending the rights of the public in the digital world. Its Web site contains a complete archive of legal documents related to *RIAA v. Verizon,* plus a long article, "RIAA v The People: Five Years Later," that presents a detailed history of the case and its consequences.

## Federal Bureau of Investigation (FBI) Cyber Investigations
J. Edgar Hoover Bldg., Washington, DC  20535-0001
(202) 324-3000
Web site: www.fbi.gov/cyberinvest/cyberhome.htm

The FBI's Web site contains official FBI information about combating cybercrime, how it is investigated, and how people can protect themselves against it. The Web site also includes articles about cases the FBI has dealt with.

**National Center for Justice and the Rule of Law (NCJRL)**
PO Box 1848, University, MS  38677
(662) 915-6897 • fax: (662) 915-6933
e-mail: ncjrl@olemiss.edu
Web site: www.olemiss.edu/depts/ncjrl

The National Center for Justice and the Rule of Law is a part
of the University of Mississippi School of Law that focuses on
issues relating to the criminal justice system. The Cybercrime
Initiative section of its Web site contains extensive information about cybercrime, including the publications *Combating
Cyber Crime* and *Cyber Crime Newsletter*, among others.

**Recording Industry Association of America (RIAA)**
1025 F Street NW, 10th Floor, Washington, DC  20004
(202) 775-0101
Web site: www.riaa.org

The Recording Industry Association of America is the trade
group that represents the U.S. recording industry. Its mission
is to foster a business and legal climate that supports and promotes its members' creative and financial vitality. Its Web site
contains a downloadable guide titled "Young People, Music
and the Internet," as well as news about its efforts to combat
piracy, information for parents, and a list of legal music sites.
There is also a FAQ for students.

**United States Department of Justice, Computer Crime
and Intellectual Property Section (CCIPS)**
John C. Keeney Bldg., Suite 600, Washington, DC  20530
(202) 514-1026 • fax: (202) 514-6113
Web site: www.cybercrime.gov

The Computer Crime and Intellectual Property Section is the
U.S. agency responsible for implementing the Department of
Justice's national strategies in combating computer and intellectual property crimes worldwide. Its Web site contains information about its policy and programs, speeches, congressional
testimony, and press releases about specific cybercrime cases.

# For Further Research

## Books

Frank W. Abagnale, *Stealing Your Life: The Ultimate Identity Theft Prevention Plan*. New York: Broadway Books, 2007.

J.M. Balkin et al., eds., *Cybercrime: Digital Cops in a Networked Environment*. New York: New York University Press, 2007.

Marjie T. Britz, *Computer Forensics and Cyber Crime: An Introduction*. Upper Saddle River, NJ: Prentice Hall, 2009.

Raoul Chiesa, Stefania Ducci, and Silvio Ciappi, *Profiling Hackers: The Science of Criminal Profiling as Applied to the World of Hacking*. Boca Raton, FL: Auerbach, 2008.

Felicia Donovan and Kristyn Bernier, *Cyber Crime Fighters: Tales from the Trenches*. Indianapolis: Que, 2008.

Charles Doyle, *Cybercrime and Its Implications*. Hauppauge, NY: Nova Science, 2009.

Danny Goodman, *Spam Wars: Our Last Best Chance to Defeat Spammers, Scammers and Hackers*. New York: Select Books, 2004.

Phillip Hallam-Baker, *The dotCrime Manifesto: How to Stop Internet Crime*. Upper Saddle River, NJ: Addison-Wesley, 2008.

Lance James, *Phishing Exposed*. Rockland, MA: Syngress, 2005.

Michael Knetzger and Jeremy Muraski, *Investigating High-Tech Crime*. Upper Saddle River, NJ: Prentice Hall, 2007.

Matt Mason, *The Pirate's Dilemma: How Youth Culture Is Reinventing Capitalism.* New York: Free Press, 2008.

Megan M. McNally and Graeme R. Newman, eds., *Perspectives on Identity Theft.* Monsey, NY: Criminal Justice Press, 2008.

Samuel C. McQuade, ed. *Encyclopedia of Cybercrime.* Westport, CT: Greenwood, 2008.

H. Thomas Milhorn, *Cybercrime: How to Avoid Becoming a Victim.* Boca Raton, FL: Universal, 2007.

Kevin D. Mitnick and William L. Simon, *The Art of Intrusion: The Real Stories Behind the Exploits of Hackers, Intruders and Deceivers.* Indianapolis: Wiley, 2005.

Robert O'Harrow, *No Place to Hide.* New York: Free Press, 2006.

Bernadette H. Schell and Clemens Martin, *Cybercrime: A Reference Handbook.* Santa Barbara, CA: ABC-CLIO, 2004.

Bruce Schneier, *Secrets and Lies: Digital Security in a Networked World.* New York: Wiley, 2004.

Debra Littlejohn Shinder and Michael Cross, *Scene of the Cybercrime.* Burlington, MA: Syngress, 2008.

David S. Wall, *Cybercrime: The Transformation of Crime in the Information Age.* Malden, MA: Polity, 2007.

Peter Warren and Michael Streeter, *Cyber Alert: How the World Is Under Attack from a New Form of Crime.* London: Vision, 2005.

## Periodicals

Tony Aeilts, "Defending Against Cybercrime and Terrorism," *FBI Law Enforcement Bulletin,* January 2005.

*Consumer Reports*, "Prescription for Trouble," February 2001.

———, "Protect Yourself Online," September 2008.

Simon Dumenco, "Robot Nudity," *New York*, August 25, 2003.

*Economist*, "Dusting for Digital Fingerprints," March 12, 2005.

———, "Fighting the Worms of Mass Destruction," November 29, 2003.

Dennis Fisher, "Tales of Cybercrime," *eWeek*, May 24, 2004.

Andrea Foster, "Appeals Court, Allowing Warrantless Search, Clarifies Online-Privacy Rights," *Chronicle of Higher Education*, April 20, 2007.

———, "Court Slows Efforts to Stop Illegal Sharing of Music," *Chronicle of Higher Education*, January 9, 2004.

Mark Frank, "Foiling Cyberbullies in the New Wild West," *Educational Leadership*, December 2005/January 2006.

*GAO Reports*, "File Sharing Programs: The Use of Peer-to-Peer Networks to Access Pornography," May 25, 2005.

Pam Greenberg, "Spam Slam: Virginia's Anti-Spam Law," *State Legislatures*, December 2005.

Larry Greenemeier, "To Catch a Hacker," *InformationWeek*, May 15, 2006.

Larry Greenemeier and J. Nicholas Hoover, "The Hacker Economy," *Information Week*, February 12, 2007.

Linda Greenhouse, "Justices Hear Arguments on Internet Pornography Law," *New York Times*, October 31, 2007.

Bill Greenwood, "Campus Crackdown: Law Targets Music Pirates," *Information Today*, February 2009.

Brian Grow and Jason Bush, "Hacker Hunters," *Business Week*, May 30, 2005.

Joe Hernick, "Beware the Copyright Cops," *Information Week*, January 28, 2008.

Doug Johnson, "Staying Safe on the Read-Write Web," *Library Media Connection*, March 2008.

Steven Levy et al., "Courthouse Rock," *Newsweek*, September 22, 2003.

Samuel C. McQuade III, "We Must Educate Young People About Cybercrime Before They Start College," *Chronicle of Higher Education*, January 5, 2007.

Robert L. Mitchell, "Making a Federal Case," *Computerworld*, July 31, 2006.

Warren Richey, "Is Child-Porn Law Too Broad?" *Christian Science Monitor*, October 30, 2007.

Candace Rondeaux, "Anti-Spam Conviction Is Upheld," *Washington Post*, September 6, 2006.

Linda Rosencrance, "Los Alamos Worker Indicted in Hacking Incidents at Six Companies," *Computerworld*, January 11, 2001.

Michael Specter, "Damn Spam," *New Yorker*, August 6, 2007.

Gene Stephens, "Cybercrime in the Year 2025," *Futurist*, July/August 2008.

David Stout, "Supreme Court Upholds Child Pornography Law," *New York Times*, May 20, 2008.

*Supreme Court Debates*, "Is the PROTECT Act of 2003 Constitutional?" October 2008.

*Vibe*, "RIAA-ded!" July 2007.

Gregory C. Wilschsen, "Information Security: Emerging Cybersecurity Issues Threaten Federal Information Systems," *GAO Reports*, May 13, 2005.

## Internet Sources

Andra Coberly, "Fort Collins Psychiatrist Embroiled in Ground-Breaking Criminal Case," *Greeley (CO) Tribune*, January 20, 2008. www.greeleytribune.com.

Corinne Iozzio, "The Cyber Crime Hall of Fame," *PCMag.com*, September 8, 2008. www.pcmag.com.

# Index